AGRICOLA

and

Roman Britain

is one of the volumes
in the

TEACH YOURSELF HISTORY LIBRARY

Edited by A. L. ROWSE

Teach Yourself History

AGRICOLA

and

Roman Britain

by
ANDREW ROBERT BURN

Senior Lecturer in Ancient History in the University
of Glasgow; Author of *The World of Hesiod,*
The Romans in Britain, etc.

THE ENGLISH UNIVERSITIES PRESS LTD
102 NEWGATE STREET
LONDON E.C.1

To

A. C. Martindale

ÆGVSTÆ
CÆLIÆ
SORORI

FIRST PRINTED 1953
SECOND IMPRESSION 1965

PRINTED AND BOUND IN ENGLAND
FOR THE ENGLISH UNIVERSITIES PRESS LTD
BY HAZELL WATSON AND VINEY LTD, AYLESBURY

A General Introduction
to the Series

THIS series has been undertaken in the conviction that there can be no subject of study more important than history. Great as have been the conquests of natural science in our time—such that many think of ours as a scientific age *par excellence*—it is even more urgent and necessary that advances should be made in the social sciences, if we are to gain control of the forces of nature loosed upon us. The bed out of which all the social sciences spring is history; there they find, in greater or lesser degree, subject-matter and material, verification or contradiction.

There is no end to what we can learn from history, if only we would, for it is coterminous with life. Its special field is the life of man in society, and at every point we can learn vicariously from the experience of others before us in history.

To take one point only—the understanding of politics: how can we hope to understand the world of affairs around us if we do not know how it came to be what it is? How to understand Germany, or Soviet Russia, or the United States—or ourselves, without knowing something of their history?

There is no subject that is more useful, or indeed indispensable.

Some evidence of the growing awareness of this may be seen in the immense increase in the interest of the reading public in history, and the much larger place the subject has come to take in education in our time.

This series has been planned to meet the needs and demands of a very wide public and of education—they are indeed the same. I am convinced that the most congenial, as well as the most concrete and practical approach to history is the biographical, through the lives of the great men whose actions have been so much part of history, and whose careers in turn have been so moulded and formed by events.

The key idea of this series, and what distinguishes it from any other that has appeared, is the intention by way of a biography of a great man to open up a significant historical theme; for example, Cromwell and the Puritan Revolution, or Lenin and the Russian Revolution.

My hope is, in the end, as the series fills out and completes itself, by a sufficient number of biographies to cover whole periods and subjects in that way. To give you the history of the United States, for example, or the British Empire or France, *via* a number of biographies of their leading historical figures.

That should be something new, as well as convenient and practical, in education.

I need hardly say that I am a strong believer in people with good academic standards writing once more for the general reading public, and of the public being given the best that the universities can provide. From this point of view this series is intended to bring the university into the homes of the people.

A. L. ROWSE.

ALL SOULS COLLEGE,
    OXFORD.

Foreword

NO one has ever maintained that Agricola, the subject of this book, was a man who dominated his epoch or altered the course of history. The interest of his career lies, on the contrary, in its very normality. Agricola was a typical member of that Roman governing class in the best days of the empire, who bore rule from the Clyde to the Euphrates under good or bad Cæsars. The inscriptions on their monuments tell us the successive official appointments of scores of such men, revealing incidentally how typical Agricola's career was; but of him almost alone we can add personal details, and see something of the disappointments as well as the splendours of an official career. Of him alone we possess a formal biography.

Why, then, it may well be asked, write a new one?

The answer is that one can usefully add, for the modern reader, some account of the Roman background: of the Roman Army, and of the social and political history, and of many routine matters which Tacitus omits as well known to all. Partly from inscriptions, partly from literature, one can give some account of many of his colleagues and contemporaries. Lastly, but not least for an English-reading public, one can add, by the help of archæology, of inscriptions and of Roman geographical writers, something about the topography of Roman Britain and of Agricola's campaigns, which were matters of no interest to Tacitus' original readers. Very varied sources have been laid under contribution; and where in details we are thrown back on imagination (under strict control from the evidence), I have, I believe, made it quite clear just how far the evidence goes.

The debts of a book like the present one are many and various. Every book is to some extent a co-operative work —even a poet is indebted to those who have fed, clothed and educated him, as well as to those who have brought his language to the point at which he takes it up—but the debts of an ancient historian are both greater and more obvious. Every new book on Roman Britain is based on a coral-reef of earlier work, reaching back, even without mentioning ancient sources, to pioneers like George Buchanan, Camden and Horsley, and including, within living memory, the work of a host of archæologists and epigraphists since the days of the great Haverfield, the father of the modern and scientific study of Roman Britain.

Here, more particularly and personally, I wish to thank four archæologists and scholars who have read this book in proof or typescript: Professor I. A. Richmond, Lt.-Col. E. B. Birley, Master of Hatfield College, Durham, Mr. John Clarke, Rector of Paisley Grammar School, and Miss Anne Robertson of the Hunterian Museum in Glasgow. All of them have contributed by their own excavations to the present state of knowledge concerning Roman operations in Scotland; to their advice and criticism, based on intimate first-hand knowledge of the subject, the book is deeply indebted; while it is in no wise merely conventional to say that for any faults which remain they share no responsibility. The writer is also happy to acknowledge that he has learned much from all of them, both by way of the printed word and from lectures and conversation.

Among other archæologists than those named above or in the all-too-brief bibliographical note, I cannot forbear to mention Mr. W. A. Anderson, of Paisley, who, by his patient work on a flood-ravaged and consequently unsatisfactory site, confirmed the previously only rumoured existence of an Agricolan fort at Bochastle, near Callander, and thereby contributed a link to the chain of evidence on which I support my view of the strategy both of Agricola and of his opponents during his invasion of the north; and among other scholars, the late J. G. C. Anderson, of Christ Church, Oxford, sometime my tutor. I name him *honoris causa*—feeling all the more bound to do so since I have gradually parted company from practically all his views.

FOREWORD

My thanks are due also to my wife, who found time in the midst of housekeeping both to type a manuscript which would have defeated many professionals and also to collaborate in the pruning and simplification of many a refractory paragraph.

ARB —1*

Contents

Chapter One

Forum Julii

AGRICOLA and his mother lived first at Forum Julii, between the sea and the mountains, on the coast of Provence. From the top of the walls, one looked over the glittering waves or the sapphire blue of a calm. It was only comparatively rarely grey, cold and rain-whipped, like the seas that Agricola later came to know so well in the north. West, north and north-east, one looked over miles of rich alluvial plain, orchards and vineyards, and cornland between grey olive-trees—to the wooded hills, green in clear weather or grey and purple in the summer haze. That plain was where the family lands were; broad lands—the family had prospered in the three generations since the veterans of Julius Cæsar's VIIIth Legion were established on smallholdings there (the usual Roman method of providing for the ex-service man), and the little town became a Roman borough, bearing Cæsar's name. Down the other way, at the waterside, at the foot of the rocky knoll on which the town was built, were big government installations, no doubt quite as interesting to a smart little boy as the stables at the home-farm : the dockyard, with room for building a dozen war-galleys at a time; the great vaulted store-buildings, with the commandant's house conveniently built on top of the vaults and on a level with the streets of the town; the fortified war-harbour, with only one narrow entrance between its two stone moles. But there was not much life down there now. One had to pretend; for the base had been closed after fifty years of activity, and was on a caretaker basis, if not actually beginning to moulder. In an advanced state of decay, one can see it still : the vaults yawning open, with a jungle of blackberry thorn blocking their entrance and rooting dangerously in the walls; the commandant's house with walls almost gone and grass disrupting its tessellated floors; the harbour between its moles a vegetable garden. For the busy waters of the Rivers Argens and Reyran, which already before the dawn of history had turned the knoll of Fréjus from an island into a promontory, have now turned the promontory into a hillock nearly a mile from the sea.

The construction of the naval base dated from the time of Cæsar Augustus, then a tremendous name in the recent past: a Napoleon, who had ridden the storm of revolution, and who then, by tact and compromise, had stabilised his position and added to the glamour of his name something of the moral prestige of a Queen Victoria. Augustus had established the base here, well back out of reach of the enemy, when he was training his young navy to fight Cleopatra, Queen of Egypt, and Mark Antony, the rival warlord, who (as all the history books said) had gone over to her and planned to make her mistress of Rome, reigning at his side.

Forum Julii, though not an ancient town, had certainly plenty of history. Its very name recalled that of Cæsar, its founder; and the first mention of it which we have is appropriate to its origin. It comes from the dramatic May days of the year after Cæsar's death, in a letter to Rome from the local army commander. For it was there on the road from Italy, at the crossing of the Silver River, that in effect the Roman republic fell and the power of future Cæsars was established, by the refusal of the armies in Gaul to draw the sword against Cæsar's friends, in order to make the world safe for a governing class represented by Cæsar's murderers.

So there were exciting answers to every question a bright little boy could ask about the place where he lived. Even Agricola's family name was Julius; which almost certainly means that his great-great-grandfather had received Roman citizenship from Cæsar. Cæsar, during that great special command in the frontier provinces, from Gaul through northern Italy to Dalmatia, which was his stepping-stone to supreme power, had recruited freely for his legions, especially in north Italy, Gaul Within the Alps as it was called—the land inhabited by the Celtic tribes whose forebears had once sacked Rome. Legions, as opposed to native auxiliary regiments, were supposed to be recruited from Roman citizens only; but as a Roman proconsul had wide powers to grant citizenship, a little thing like that was not likely to stop a Cæsar. He, the patrician black sheep, was never much of a sympathiser with Roman bourgeois prejudices; and, the better to secure their political and military support, he extended citizen rights widely among the settled and civilised communities from the Po to the Alps.

This was the origin of the enormous numbers of Julii who appear all over the western provinces under the empire; for new citizens always took their patron's clanname. At Fréjus itself, of twenty-two families named on surviving tombstones, eight are called Julius. The sample is too small for statistical accuracy, but it is probably a fair inference that that was actually the name of about one-third of the population. Since there were also only about thirty Roman first names current, and several of these were little used or ran in families, all the more importance attached to the name which Romans wrote last, such as Agricola or, his father's third name, Græcinus. Such names had originally been given in primitive Rome as nicknames to distinguish, say, one Gaius Julius from another, and were often highly personal, meaning such things as Nosy or Fatty or Ginger. Some, like our surnames, had become fixed in families, e.g. Cæsar (perhaps "Fairhair") in a family of the patrician Julii; but this was not universal, and increasingly under the empire the third name came to be personal and individual.

Another question for the child Agricola to ask in due course was why he had no father; but to answer that, it will be best to follow further the history of his family and of the society which produced him.

Forum Julii was by no means the only settlement of old soldiers in its region. There was a constellation of them, scattered right across the Old Province in southern France: men of the Second Legion at Orange, of the Sixth at Arles, of the famous Tenth at Narbonne and so on. They and their sons proceeded to equip their cities with the amenities of Roman life: theatres, amphitheatres (some used today for bull-fighting), good water from aqueducts such as the magnificent Pont du Gard near Nîmes, triumphal arches, adorned with scenes of battle and sculptured trophies of captured Gallic arms. There was no tenderness for the susceptibilities of the conquered. One monument, of which a fragment is in the museum at Narbonne, shows Roman soldiers effecting an opposed landing. Since there are no notable river-battles in Cæsar's campaigns, one wonders, is it the Tenth Legion landing in Britain?

One wonders also where all the labour came from to carry out so many works in one generation; and the answer probably is that much of the heavy hauling and lifting was done by the slave-labour of Gallic and German prisoners of war.

Thus Provence became, as was said in Agricola's time, less a province than an extension of Italy; though, as we saw, many of the soldier-colonists must have been of Celtic descent. Fréjus was not one of the most opulent of these colonies; in fact, rather a modest place compared with Nîmes or Arles. Its walls, aqueduct and public buildings were of brick, no good stone for large buildings being locally available; and the theatre had not a quarter the seating capacity of the huge structure at Orange. After the naval base was closed, it must have been a quiet little place, enlivened only by its position on the coast road from Italy. But it was well known for its amenities—good air, good water, good milk and the other produce of its fertile plain. They are all mentioned in a letter which Pliny, a younger friend of Agricola's family, wrote to a mutual friend, asking leave to send a sick slave to Fréjus to convalesce on the friend's estates. It was a pleasant, perhaps sleepy, country town, whose history had moved on and left it; but typical of those provincial boroughs whose decent, sober, perhaps rather dull, society contrasted favourably in point of morals with that of the capital. So say all Roman moralists, in general terms; so says Tacitus, Agricola's son-in-law, explicitly referring to his hero's youth in Provence;

and the stable and affectionate middle-class family life
revealed by the tombstones in hundreds of Roman ceme-
teries confirms their warning that one must not judge the
whole Roman empire by what Tacitus, in another vein,
says of the court of Nero.

From these military colonies, in Spain, Gaul and the
Danube countries, in Africa and the east, came a high proportion of the legionaries who conquered Britain and
guarded the Rhine and Danube and the desert frontiers
in Africa and Syria. Only a few came from central and
southern Italy, where the old population continually
failed to replace itself, to the distress and anxiety of the
government. The gaps were filled up by swarms of
foreign workers, recruited through the slave-market or
born in the slaves' quarters, thousands of whom in each
generation became freedmen and the parents of full
citizens. It is rare for a population to be destroyed as a
result of foreign conquest; but it really does seem that the
population of ancient Rome largely disappeared as the
result of conquering others, to be replaced by the descendants of its own slaves. But already in the first century one result of the recruitment of Cæsar's legions among
the poorer citizens and among the new citizens made itself
felt. The soldiers and many of the regimental officers and
government officials were conscious of being Cæsar's men;
Julii even by name, no small number of them. If they
came from the military colonies, they came of families
which owed their fields and often their citizenship to
Cæsar. If they had no lands yet, they looked to the reigning Cæsar to provide for their old age. This is one reason
why, though there was still much academic republican
sentiment among members of the old families at Rome,
and though there was talk of restoring the republic almost
whenever an early Cæsar was murdered, such talk never
came to anything. Physical force was in the hands of the
new class, the men of Cæsar's revolution.

At the colonies themselves, naturally, society did not
stand still. Some ex-legionaries made good farmers; many,
it was notorious, did not. Their failure was not necessarily
a source of unmixed grief to their more successful neigh-

bours. If some grew poor, many prospered; there were great advantages in being a Roman citizen. There was also the Service for younger sons, with a fair chance, for the citizen recruit, of rising to be a company commander —a centurion. Also, in the early days, as we saw, rough slave labour was cheap—Gauls, Germans, Spanish Galicians, later again Britons, from the aggressive wars of the early Cæsars.

Centurions, in particular, often grew quite rich; they had numerous ways of extorting a rake-off from the meagre pay of their men. Later, in Agricola's lifetime, the centurions' pay was greatly increased and these perquisites were forbidden. And for a few hand-picked centurions—as also for the sons of many, if they could show substantial property, a fair education, and a recommendation from a highly placed patron, say a general or governor—there opened a still more resplendent prospect, as a member of the second-highest grade of the emperor's service. Members of this grade were called *procurators* (whence our terms proctor and procurator fiscal); a word simply meaning agent or commissioner. Such agents of the emperor filled a vast range of posts, financial and administrative, looking after mines, ranches, farms, survey offices and other details of the emperor's huge properties (including much former property of defeated rebels) scattered through the empire. One such estate—the largest of them all, by far— was Egypt; to be Prefect of Egypt was the pinnacle of the most successful and trusted procurator's career. Other senior procurators held posts of chief revenue-collecting officer of a province, responsible not to the governor but directly to the emperor; and some were themselves governors of small provinces, usually in special and rather difficult areas. There were three such districts in the Alps, for instance. Another was Judæa, where one Pontius Pilate unwittingly became the most famous procurator in history.

For appointment to any of these posts there was, as mentioned above, a stiff property qualification: that of a "knight"—the class who, in the old citizen army, would have had the right and duty of serving, with their own horses, as cavalry. One had to show property valued at

400,000 sesterces, a sum which—since neither Roman nor modern money remains perfectly stable in value—is best "translated" by being related to the standard daily wage of a workman. The sesterce was a heavy bronze coin of the weight of about two and a half pennies; but to reckon from this (as used to be done in the days when £1 meant a gold sovereign) that 100 sesterces = £1 was not really sensible even in 1880. Four sesterces made a denarius or "penny"—a small silver piece like a Swiss franc—and a "penny", as in the parable of the Labourers in the Vineyard, was the highest daily wage paid for unskilled labour. Casual labourers did not get it every day—they might, as in the parable, find themselves standing in the market-place "all the day idle". The minimum property of a "knight" therefore represented the equivalent of pay for 100,000 man-days of manual labour.

The imperial hierarchy was based, that is to say, on the social classes of a very lofty social pyramid. All senior officers and officials were very rich men—some of them, of course, possessed many times the necessary minimum. It is important to recognise this, because these immense inequalities of wealth account for many characteristics of Roman life: the prodigious extravagances of smart society, the avarice, the vast prices paid for town houses or for beautiful slaves and other luxury goods, and, on the other hand, the "bread and circuses", the costly shows, the expenditure on free bread for poor citizens at Rome, and the daily disbursements by rich men to hordes of often entirely undeserving citizen "clients". These institutions took, in an ill-organised and sometimes thoroughly pernicious way, the place of social services; but they benefited, chiefly, not productive workers but lazy and parasitic Roman citizens.

These extravagances and evils, however, were only seen at their worst in Rome itself and in some of the large towns of the Greek-speaking east. The military colonies, lately founded as the markets and centres of self-administering farming communities, were relatively free from them; and from these and other western provincial municipalities, as the first century of our era proceeded and the rule of the

7

Cæsars settled into a system, there came up to Rome a steady stream of intelligent, self-respecting, upright men, mostly the sons of families successful at home and now launching out to seek fame in the great world. They included most of the best-known literary men of the new age, many of its best public servants and administrators, and the ancestors of many emperors. Of such, then, were Agricola's forebears.

The first of whom we know anything personally was Agricola's grandfather. Rich enough to gain entry to the "knightly" class, he rose, in the later years of Augustus' long reign, to be a procurator—one of the "aristocrats of the equestrian class" says Tacitus with the faintest trace of a sniff. (Tacitus, probably himself a procurator's son, had risen a class higher.) Among other posts, he served for some years in the Rhineland. He appears in an anecdote quoted by his son as a shrewd and kindly observer of the world about him; and he laid the foundation for that son's brilliant though, as it proved, cruelly short career.

Lucius Julius Græcinus, Agricola's father, was in his day one of the most brilliant younger members of the Roman Senate. He owed it, no doubt, to his own father that he received, like many a centurion's son, the Latin and Greek literary education of a Roman gentleman. The third name of Græcinus, "the Grecian", if as is likely his father chose it, reflects the old procurator's enthusiasm for Greek culture, of which Marseilles and her daughter colonies on the coast of Provence were the missionaries and outposts. But it must have been a tribute to Lucius' own promise, as well as to his father's efficient and loyal service, that Tiberius, the successor of Augustus and himself a veteran administrator, accepted him for a cadetship in the highest grade of the imperial service, membership of which gave, after about three years, a seat in the ancient council of state, the Roman Senate. There were only twenty vacancies in this grade of the service each year, and first preference always went to senators' sons. The fact that the Senate never kept up its own numbers by natural increase, however, meant that there were often a few vacancies for sons of knights; and it must have been the highest ambition

8

of many a procurator to see his son chosen for one of
them.

Lucius Græcinus at Rome won many friends, and was
remembered as a wit, a man of letters and a man whose
ethical standards impressed contemporaries. It was remembered, for instance, that when he held the office of prætor,
and when friends, real and "official", were subscribing towards the cost of the public entertainments expected of
him in that position, he actually declined one subscription
because the donor was a man of bad character—and then
another for the same reason, with the bland excuse, "I did
not accept one from Persicus either". He was adored by his
young wife, Agricola's mother. She was from Provence, the
daughter of another procurator (and yet another Julius)
who had land at Ventimiglia, twenty miles east of Fréjus.
Her name was Julia Procilla; the latter name was common
in Gaul, and is perhaps another indication of Celtic
descent. She may have been Lucius' second wife; for a
recently discovered inscription at Rome appears to be a
memorial to him set up by a hitherto unknown son, Marcus Julius Græcinus; and since Marcus plays no part in
Tacitus' life of Agricola, it has been thought that he was a
half-brother. He was probably much older than Agricola,
and may (since nothing else is heard of him) have died
before Agricola was grown up and began his public career.

Lucius Græcinus, as a rising and respected senator,
seemed destined for a distinguished middle age; but
disaster was impending. In A.D. 37, three years before the
birth of Agricola, Tiberius died, old, suspicious (especially since the discovery that one of his chief ministers was
plotting to supplant him), aloof and unpopular. The new
emperor, Gaius, his great-nephew, seemed likely to be a
great improvement; but Gaius shortly showed himself to
be autocratic and suspicious in his turn, and a reign of
terror developed. Gaius became jealous of his father-in-
law, Silanus, an ex-Proconsul of Africa, and desired
Græcinus to prosecute him for treason. Græcinus had the
great courage to refuse. Nothing happened to him immediately; other prosecutors were found, and Silanus
committed suicide early in 38. But it was evident that,

at least under Gaius, Græcinus' official career was at an end.

This, then, was why Græcinus' son was born at Fréjus, and not either at Rome or in the governor's house in a province.

Græcinus in disgrace behaved with the dignity of a man who lived his philosophy. Untheatrically, he retired to his estates and employed his leisure in writing. There were not many possible topics for a man in the bad books of a bad Cæsar; almost everything—history, philosophy, most kinds of poetry—could not help containing passages which, wrenched from their context, might be represented by an enemy anxious to curry favour with Cæsar as comments on the régime; and everyone had enemies—the "unco' guid" probably not least. But it was an honourable tradition among Roman gentlemen to be interested in farming and capable, or at least apparently capable, of managing their own estates; and Græcinus came from a good farming district. Next to his virtues and his witticisms, he was remembered for the "scholarly charm" of his book on vines and viticulture; and the part of his career when he most obviously had time for writing is after his fall from favour.

So for some two years, one likes to think, Græcinus and Procilla lived their Stoic idyll in the pleasant land of Fréjus, cultivating their philosophic garden while the sword hung over them. As we know in our time, one can get used to anxiety. He played the Roman squire among his tenants, and they walked in their vineyards and he worked at his book—though a good deal in it, it transpires, was borrowed from a previous writer, Cornelius Celsus. In practical Roman fashion, he added figures to show how well and how steadily vine-growing paid; and among other illustrations, he told a story of his father's on the merits of intensive cultivation. A farmer in the Rhineland had two daughters and a modest holding given up to vine growing. When the elder daughter married, he gave her a third of his land as dowry; but by devoting more attention to the remainder, he made as large an income as before. Then, when the younger daughter married, he heroically gave her half the remainder, and by intensive cultivation still found himself not appreciably poorer.

At Fréjus, on the 13th June, A.D. 40, their son was born, and named Gnæus Julius Agricola. Agricola means Farmer. It was a common practice—a Greek practice, more than a Roman one—to name a son, if not after an ancestor, then after his father's interests or occupation. Agricola was a more prosaic name than Græcinus; but Græcinus had been a "Grecian", a philosopher and an idealist; and it did not appear, in the long run, to have been profitable.

The young emperor, Gaius Caligula, went from bad to worse. He was at daggers drawn with the senate, suspecting half its members of republicanism. They for their part took their revenge by deciding that he was quite mad, and circulating parodied accounts of his every action, which have found their way into our history books. In the summer of 40 he was in Gaul, preparing an invasion of Britain, where quarrels between the sons of the late King Cymbeline and the flight of one of them to the Romans gave Rome an excuse for intervention; but at the last moment Gaius called off the expedition. The hostile account has it that, incapable of sticking to any policy for long, he suddenly ordered his troops to fall out and pick up shells on the beach, informing them that these were "spoils of the ocean". The fact may be that, convinced of widespread disaffection among his officers, he felt that he could not afford a long absence overseas, and did not wish to give military glory to one of his generals. There had already been serious enough conspiracies against him; and about this time—probably after rather than before the birth of Agricola—something, or some toady and informer, reminded him of Græcinus.

We know nothing about the immediate circumstances of the tragedy. Emperors in fear of conspirators gave no account of their actions. Gaius, angry and thwarted, on his way back to Rome must needs pass through Provence, and nothing would be easier than to send a squad of military police to execute a suspect. Græcinus perished, says the philosopher Seneca, who had known him, because he was too good a man for his existence to be in the interests of a tyrant. So Julia Procilla was left a widow, and Gaius returned to Rome, to fall in the next year by the hands of a group of his servants under an officer whom he had insulted.

Julia took over the management of her estates and devoted herself to bringing up the little Agricola. Tacitus speaks of her as "a lady of rare chastity", which may sound to the modern ear like an insult to other Roman ladies, but is not meant as such. His point is that she was still young, evidently well-to-do, and could easily have married again. But for her, who had been the wife of Græcinus, there could be no other man.

Chapter Two

School at Marseilles, and
News from Britain (A.D. 43–60)

NOT long after, in the interests of Agricola's education and doubtless also to escape from painful associations, Julia moved to Marseilles.

Marseilles (Massilia to the Romans) was already an ancient town. For over six hundred years its temples and fortress walls had crowned the citadel above its harbour— ever since the bold Greek sailors of Phokaia in Asia Minor had made their way here in search of silver and tin, and one of their young leaders had married a Celtic or pre-Celtic king's daughter and founded the settlement. A long and brilliant history had followed. Holding her own with her fleet against Phœnician Carthage, though at one time almost cut off from the Greek world, Massilia had survived, grown and prospered, spreading her daughter colonies along the coast from Spain to the wild Riviera, where the name of Nice (Nicæa, "the Victorious") commemorates a success perhaps against the Etruscans. Government was in the hands of a prudent oligarchy, which knew better than to misgovern its workmen and sailors: a Council of Six Hundred land-owners, merchants and bankers and an executive "cabinet" of fifteen. Spanish silver came in through Ampurias, "the emporium"; tin through the native fortress of Enserune near Béziers, which grew rich on the proceeds—just where the Canal du Midi, the earliest great canal of modern Europe, now starts its journey to the Atlantic by the primeval route through Narbonne and Carcassonne.

As to where the tin came from, that long remained a secret. Rumours spoke of Tin Islands somewhere in the

Atlantic (not necessarily the same islands in all centuries);
but Carthage kept the Straits of Gibraltar closed to inter-
lopers. Only rarely, perhaps when Carthage was at war
with the Greeks of Sicily, could explorers slip through.
Euthymenes of Marseilles reached south to the Senegal; his
compatriot Pytheas was the discoverer of Britain, and gave
a detailed account of its coasts, estuaries and natural
phenomena. But Carthage recovered again; Pytheas' voyage
could not be or at least was not repeated; and his reports
of light summer nights, high tides, including the Severn
bore, and perhaps of the Arctic Ocean were so astonishing
to Mediterranean sailors that this very great explorer was
dismissed by indoor geographers as a very great liar.

Massilia first came into Rome's orbit as an honoured
ally against Carthage. At the end of the republic she supported the government against Cæsar, and stood a siege,
during which her troops treacherously attacked Cæsar's
men during an armistice. It was, to say the least, a
costly miscalculation. Marseilles' broad lands in the interior went to swell the provision made for Cæsar's
veterans. But under the Empire, if her heroic age was past,
the city still prospered; much shipping still used the harbour, despite the existence of a canal through the Rhone
delta to Arles; and, above all, Massilia had an old tradition of culture, as befitted the great outpost of that Greek
world which was to the Romans as Europe to modern
America. As young men from Rome went to Athens, or
sometimes to Rhodes, to study Greek thought and literature with Greek masters, so young Romans of Gaul, and
Gallic chieftains' sons also, went to study at Marseilles.
At all three there were teachers of all the liberal arts:
grammar, poetry and public speaking; mathematics,
astronomy and the nature of the physical world; logic,
metaphysics and ethics. There were renowned professors
who charged highly for admission to their lectures, and
lesser lights who for a moderate charge might be booked
for seminars and tutorials. There were no organised universities, but all three cities must have had much the air
of a university town. Young men more or less actively pur-
suing their studies formed a recognisable element in their

populations; well-to-do young men, most of them, attended by their own servants like young eighteenth-century noblemen. The pressure of work was not high, and hunting parties, gambling, concerts, the theatre and the other occupations of a rich young man's social life filled up a good deal of the time. There were no examinations, and the chief worry of many of them must have been an occasional letter from father, as from Cicero to his son at Athens in an earlier generation, suspicious that young Marcus was getting through too much money and not doing much work. Agricola as a young man was one of the steadier characters.

At his mother's house at Marseilles, then, varied no doubt with visits to the family's estates and to the country-houses of friends in Provence, Agricola spent his youth. But while he was still a child the events began which were ultimately to shape his life. When he was only three, the Emperor Claudius' expeditionary force landed in Britain.

Just on a hundred years had passed—ninety-seven, to be exact—since Julius Cæsar's raids had made the name of Britain familiar to "a wider public"; and during that time Roman military and financial circles had never wholly ceased to dream of the conquest. Horace in his patriotic poems had referred to it as imminent; and though the project had been shelved during Augustus' German wars and Tiberius' régime of peace and retrenchment, the Emperor Gaius had promptly taken it up again.

Motives for undertaking the invasion were various and powerful. First, Roman wars of conquest were relatively inexpensive—there was no heavy bill for ammunition, and the army had to be fed anyhow—and they were definitely profitable to those who planned and led the campaigns. Britain was reported to be rich in metals and in pearls from the Richborough oyster-beds; and though both the pearls and the rumoured gold- and silver-mines proved disappointing, the lead, tin and iron ore were real enough. Scarcely less important was the prospect of cheap slave labour, with which both British and continental mines and farms could be worked. Roman knights, the great business class, looked for new procuratorships and openings in

trade; senators, who were debarred from trade, were by no
means debarred from making loans out of their surplus
wealth. And for plain soldiers, though some of them were
at first distinctly nervous at the prospect of fighting in this
"other world", there was of course the consoling prospect
of plain loot. Add to this that a free Britain could harbour Celtic malcontents from Gaul, and was a "bad
example", and that the new emperor, Claudius, a stam-
mering, middle-aged uncle of Gaius, who had been kept in
the background and had consoled himself with historical
studies, promptly evinced a craving for real military glory
now that he had the chance of it; and the invasion of
Britain followed almost inevitably.

In Britain itself, meanwhile, things had not stood still.
Cassivellaunus, king of the Belgian Catuvellauni of Hert-
fordshire, who had fought the great Cæsar with determina-
tion and resource, had resumed his career of conquest in
Britain after Cæsar had gone. His son or grandson
Tasciovanus followed in his steps; and *his* son Cunobelinus,
Shakespeare's Cymbeline, conquered the Trinovantes in
Essex, who had been saved from Cassivellaunus by
Cæsar's intervention, and transferred his court and his
chief mint to Colchester, the Trinovantian capital. Two
unsuccessful rivals, Tincommius and Dumnovellaunus,
fled to Rome and appealed to Augustus, who complacently
recorded the appeal as evidence of his own influence, but
did nothing to restore them.

Cymbeline was the most powerful prince Britain had
ever seen. The distribution of his coins, and of those of
other British kingdoms, shows his territory extending far
across the midlands; the Dobunni of the Cotswolds
trembled in their hill-forts, and the tough Silures of South
Wales were prepared to be led by a son of Cymbeline in
the next generation.

Meanwhile, since the days of Cæsar, another Belgic
kingdom had spread from Southampton Water to meet
the Catuvellauni on the middle Thames—the kingdom of
the Atrebates, from Arras in Picardy. Its founder was
Commius, once the friend of Cæsar, later, when he had
seen more of Rome's methods, his bitter enemy; the first

inhabitant of Britain of whose personal adventures a few details are known. South British society, in short, was in a state of turmoil. There was much "Homeric" magnificence in the halls of kings; but the country was split by intense rivalries, between the different Belgic dynasties and even between brother princes. The splendours of late Celtic enamel- and metal-work contrasted with palisades and gates adorned with the heads of conquered enemies (an equally Homeric custom); while on all sides, and even within the Belgic world, the descendants of older peoples —slaves, serfs and tribes yet unconquered—had no love for the invaders. Slave-chains, which have been found more than once among remains of pre-Roman Britain, serve as tangible reminders that if Roman conquerors, according to Tacitus himself, were often greedy and brutal, the state of affairs on which they impinged was by no means idyllic.

This state of affairs, indeed, with the country split both by racial feuds and by incipient class divisions, and with tribal capitals offering tangible military objectives, accounts for the fact that the whole south-east went down before Claudius' generals as quickly as Gaul before Cæsar a hundred years before. The wilder and also more homogeneous tribes of Wales and the north, like those of Spain and Germany, were a very different matter; and it was not only their mountains that made them so. Even so, Caratacus (Caradoc) and Togodumnus, the sons of Cymbeline, made the Romans fight hard in Kent, holding out, especially, for two days in a severe battle on the Medway; but by the end of the first summer Colchester was occupied, the Roman Emperor coming over in person to witness the advance from the Thames; Togodumnus had fallen fighting or died of his wounds; and Caratacus, slipping, we must suppose, through the territory of the Dobunni, who were no friends of his, took refuge with the Silures in South Wales, who may well have had diplomatic relations with his family against the Dobunni in earlier days. Neighbouring kings in the south-east hastened to make their peace with Rome: King Prasutagus of the non-Belgic Iceni in Norfolk, King Cogidumnus in Sussex;

17

and, according to Roman practice, they were retained as rulers of "native states", destined for absorption later.

Claudius' general, Aulus Plautius, was thus able, in the following summers, to divide his army of four legions (plus cavalry and light infantry, some 40,000 men in all) into separate columns, and to carry out a methodical sweeping movement through Wessex and the midlands. Legion II Augusta ("The Emperor's Own"), under one Titus Flavius Vespasianus, a tax-collector's son and centurion's grandson from central Italy, who had won distinction on the Medway, carved its way in a score of little battles through the resistance of the south-western Belgæ and reached the Isle of Wight. Next came the turn of the Durotriges, in Dorset, whose great fortress of Maiden Castle was stormed, with carnage in the main gateway, the traces of which have been discovered by archæologists in modern times. On the other wing the IXth "Spanish" Legion (their title was a battle-honour dating from Cæsar's civil wars) pushed through the east midlands and before long had a permanent cantonment at Lincoln. In the centre, the XIVth and XXth reached Shropshire, hacking a way through the forests for their line of communications, which is still followed by our Holyhead Road. The XIVth lay for a time at Uriconium or Viroconium on the Severn—a name which still survives in those of Wroxeter and the Wrekin. But beyond the Severn they ran into the stern resistance of the Welsh tribes under the indomitable Caradoc. Against this, the IInd Legion also was called up from the borders of Devon to a base at Gloucester; and even so, it was long before the Romans advanced their bases beyond the Severn line.

With Caradoc at large in Wales, the Romans were in no position to fight at the same time the great northern tribe of the Brigantes, in Yorkshire and Durham; but fortunately for them this tribe also had its internal dissensions. The queen-regnant, Cartimandua, and her consort, a great warrior named Venutius, had opponents at home; and to secure their position they were not above accepting Roman assistance. Tacitus' account of Plautius' governorship is lost; but when he next mentions Venutius, in the time of

Plautius' successor, he reminds us that Venutius had *earlier* accepted Rome's alliance and armed Roman aid. Finds of apparently Claudian pottery at York are perhaps a tangible relic of this episode. Plautius was thus able to neutralise, with small forces, the most powerful tribe in Britain.

Plautius was recalled about A.D. 47, to a well-earned ovation (a kind of minor triumphal procession; the full Roman triumph was by this time reserved for emperors). His successor, P. Ostorius Scapula, consolidated his position, building the great road for lateral communication, now known as the Fosse Way. He then disarmed the tribes east of the Trent–Severn line, not without a sharp brush with the still unconquered Iceni, in which his son Marcus won the "Victoria Cross of the Roman Army"—the crown of oak leaves awarded to a soldier of any rank for saving the life of a fellow-Roman in action.

Ostorius next pushed through to the Irish Sea near Chester, nipped in the bud an anti-Roman movement among the Brigantes, and turned against Wales. There was prolonged fighting against an elusive enemy. At last Caradoc "transferred the seat of war to the land of the Ordovices", in North Wales, says Tacitus; perhaps the strain and losses of the long war that he had brought upon the Silures had shaken his position there. In this new theatre of war he gave battle to Ostorius, which again suggests that his position was shaken, and that he could no longer nerve the tribesmen to face the sufferings inseparable from a "scorched-earth" policy and a guerilla war. The inevitable disaster resulted; the Romans broke through the strongest defences which he could find—a Welsh mountain-side with a hill-fort at the top and a river at the bottom. Caradoc, seeing no future for himself in Wales, slipped away again with his personal following, through enemy territory, to attempt a last desperate coup: nothing less than to throw himself on the mercy of Queen Cartimandua, probably in the hope of persuading her that Rome was no friend to any British dynasty, and that honour and expediency demanded that she should involve her tribe in the war.

The attempt failed. Cartimandua preferred her new

allies to barbarian honour, let her suppliants walk into a trap, and delivered them to the Romans. So Caradoc was sent off with his family and followers to face the Emperor in Rome. It was A.D. 51, the ninth year of the war.

The journey through France and Italy was something of a triumphal procession, though a melancholy one for the prisoners. The fame of Caratacus, says Tacitus, had spread far and wide on the continent, and men were eager to see this champion who had for nine years defied the power of Rome. Evidently the war-news, represented by the stories of returned soldiers and perhaps by official communiqués in the larger centres, was a matter of general interest. And so we may consider it virtually certain that in Provence, probably at Marseilles, the eleven-year-old Agricola had his first sight of a British king.

Caratacus, when at last he stood unabashed and undismayed before Claudius, was humanely treated, one is glad to hear. With his wife, daughter and brothers, he was probably allowed to live out his time on parole or under open arrest somewhere in Italy. (Cæsar had kept Vercingetorix for six years in prison, to be put to death, according to the savage old Roman custom, after the dictator's victory procession.) After the hardships and excitements of the past nine years, peace and quiet may have been not unwelcome for a time. But it was not freedom.

There can be not the least doubt that the boy Agricola and his friends played at being brave Roman soldiers routing savage Britons out of their fastnesses and ambuscades; but it would not be true to represent him as dedicated from boyhood to the idea of service in Britain. He had still seven years of schooling before him, before the time came for the son of a senator to embark on his official career; and during adolescence he was for a time much more attracted by the beauties of philosophy. "Altogether too much interested in philosophy for a Roman and a senator", he used to say in after life, referring to these years; one can imagine the tones of the successful general, looking back on the young intellectual of his student days. But he always remained something of an idealist, as befitted his father's son.

Philosophy, in the Roman empire, was no longer largely concerned with natural science, as it had been in the great days of Greece, 500 years before. The confident mood bred of successful Greek expansion in the Mediterranean had faded, with the increasingly vigorous reaction of the non-Greek peoples, and also with the realisation that if the theories of almost any one of the great "physicists" were correct, all the others were very wrong indeed. With the disintegration of early Greek society and its traditional morality, and especially after the conquests of Alexander had left the city-states, no longer powerful, engulfed in a world of warring empires, the pressing problem was rather how the individual was to live and act, in a world full of frustrations and blind forces. Within the generation after Alexander two philosophies were launched, both at Athens, which grappled with this problem, and which were to divide the allegiance of most educated Greeks and Romans under the Roman empire: the philosophies of those Stoics and Epicureans with whom St. Paul was to argue on "Mars' Hill" below the Acropolis. Each of these took over from one of the "physicists" a doctrine of the nature of mind and matter as a theoretical basis for its ethics; but it was a basis and no more; a body of dogma set forth and disputed keenly enough, but in a scholastic, not a scientific, manner. Greek natural science made progress only in the hands of specialists, after the great work of Alexander's tutor, Aristotle; and some Romans—Tacitus, for example—do not seem to have understood the best astronomy of their own age.

Epicurus, founder of the Epicurean philosophy, was a gentle Athenian, who in bad days for his country discoursed to a circle of friends in his garden and taught an ethic of personal integrity and doing no harm; in that way, he said, the true pleasure of life was gained. Pleasure, indeed, was the only rational end of action; for his physics and metaphysics were materialistic. He took over the atomic theory of Democritus, a contemporary of Socrates. Spirit, he held, was merely a delicate form of matter. The world was an accident; a fleeting product, in the infinity of time, of a fortuitous concourse of atoms hurtling through space. The gods existed, but took no interest in men; their tenuous bodies dwelt in the spaces between the gross "concourses" of the worlds. There was no after-life, and, above all, no hell—a concept with which medicine-men and purveyors of ritual absolution were already very willing to terrify the pagan world. The only sensible course was to be true to one's self and one's friends, and avoid excesses. As Voltaire would put it—*"Il faudrait cultiver son jardin"*.

This almost existentialist ethic, along with the companionship of the Epicurean "Societies of Friends", seems to have come with the force of a revelation and release from superstitious terrors to not a few intelligent men. Lucretius, one of Epicurus' greatest disciples, is sometimes hailed by modern scientists as one of the great minds of antiquity. He is certainly one of Rome's greatest poets; but to treat him as an original thinker is a mistake. The atomic theory which he sets forth in sonorous verse is neither his own nor even Epicurus', but that of Democritus, adopted *en bloc* out of some philosophy manual.

But it was the Stoic school that had the greatest influence at Rome, especially among men of action. Zeno, its founder, was not a Greek, though he studied and taught at Athens. He was a Semite of Cyprus—a product, thus, of the same Hellenised Semitic world as St. Paul, and moved by the same moral earnestness. He, too, took over a physical theory from an earlier Greek: Heracleitus of Ephesus, the "Weeping Philosopher"; legend said he wept over the follies of men, while Democritus laughed at them. Heracleitus first stated the principle of the union of opposites, taken over from him by Hegel; but to this Zeno paid little attention. He found useful, rather, the doctrine that Fire is the most elemental form of matter, and that of fire all other things are transformations—both matter and energy, including the energies of spirits. Zeus, the "Father of gods and men" as the poets said, was in some fashion fire; no doubt this was understood by different Stoics in different degrees as allegory; and of fire also are the spirits of men: fiery particles, "Mind moving the mass", as in Vergil's vision of the soul's destiny; a passage which, like all Vergil's work, Roman schoolboys read and conned.

Man thus partakes, according to Zeno, in the divine Reason or Logos. To act according to reason is according to nature; and in virtue alone man finds happiness. Other things were "indifferent"; such things, that is, as riches and poverty, sickness and health, pain and pleasure, and a good or bad name in the sight of the world. Here Zeno was echoing Socrates, in whom Stoics saw the ideal wise man: "I do not think it is permitted by God that the bad man should do the good any harm; though he may kill him, of course, or imprison him or deprive him of property."

Here was a philosophy in the light of which, amid a rising tide of scepticism and religiosity, men, including emperors, could, if they would, serve the common weal; the religion, it is not too much to say, of many Roman men of action. Early Greek philosophers spoke of serving one's city; but to the Stoics, in the post-Alexandrian world, it was a metaphorical "city" of the whole world, a "Cosmopolis". Stoic language is shot through with the phraseology of the city-state, just as Christian language is with that of Greco-Persian monarchy. As the Stoic Emperor Marcus Aurelius writes a hundred years after Agricola: "The poet says [of Athens], 'Dear City of Cecrops'; and will not you say 'Dear city of God'?" The world was a city, all men fellow-citizens, to whom one owed honesty and justice; and the wise man also, the microcosm, should harmonise his soul like a well-ordered city, as in the last lines (save an appendix) of Plato's *Republic*:

(The wise man) " 'will not take part in politics, then,' said Glaucon, 'if that is what he cares for.'

" 'Oh yes, he will' [says Socrates], 'in his own city; though perhaps not in that in which he is born, except by some God-sent fortune.'

" 'I see; you mean in the city which we have just been founding in our talk, . . . for I do not think it exists anywhere on earth.'

" 'But' [says Socrates], 'perhaps it is laid up in heaven, as a pattern for him, who will, to look upon, and seeing it, to found a city in himself. But it makes no difference whether it exists or ever will exist; for he will work the works of that City, and of no other.' "

If young Agricola's dreams of devoting himself wholly to philosophy did not last long, that was not very surprising. Years of discretion supervened, says Tacitus primly, taking the line which he thinks proper. Or, as Wordsworth would have put it, the "vision splendid . . . fades into the light of common day". But the process was certainly helped by the influence of his mother. Tactful and tenacious, she kept her influence over him; she had her ambitions for him, and she also was definitely of opinion that one could have too much philosophy. Finally it was agreed that Agricola, like his father, would go into the public service (senatorial grade)—if, of course, the emperor would commission him. But there was not likely to be much difficulty about that. Old Claudius was dead by now, poisoned, according to rumour, by his third wife, Agrippina, herself a great-granddaughter of Augustus. The new emperor was that wife's son, whom Claudius had adopted; he was known by the old Claudian family name of Nero. He was a youth only a couple of years older than Agricola; a youth fond of grandiose ideas and interested in the arts, but frankly bored by the details of administration. In these circumstances, the two most influential men in Rome were two men from the provinces, both of whom had known Agricola's father. Afranius Burrus, who commanded the Guards, came from Vaison-la-Romaine in Provence; Seneca, Nero's late tutor and now his chief civil minister, from Spain. He was a brother of that Gallio who is recorded to have "cared for none of these things" during a religious riot at Corinth. Seneca was a well-known Stoic, and had known and respected Græcinus, to whose character and witticisms he refers more than once in his philosophical essays.

So to Rome, at the age of nineteen or twenty, Agricola went. It may well have been his first visit to the capital, and the buildings alone would have made that memorable. There was the vast mausoleum of Augustus beside the Tiber, with the proud record of his achievements inscribed on its walls; the temples, including the Pantheon, built by Augustus' general, Agrippa, and still a place of worship today; the public libraries, the historic Forum, the new buildings on the Capitol; the great men's houses in their own grounds, for which a satirist not long after coined the phrase *rus in urbe*; and the still larger gardens of great men of the past, which had become public parks. Less a matter for boasting, but remorselessly underlined by the same satirist, Juvenal, were some of the disamenities of a large town: the noise, the traffic-jams, the crazy six-storey tenements of the poor, which sometimes collapsed or caught fire with heavy loss of life; the habit, as in old Edinburgh, of emptying the slops, with scant warning, out of an upper window.

But Agricola was not in Rome as a mere tourist. He was on business, and much in earnest about it. He stayed, no doubt, with friends of his family. There would be no difficulty about introductions, though he would probably have to do some tedious waiting round the court on the Palatine Hill, waiting for a formal audience of the Emperor. One wonders what he thought of Nero; probably—it would occur to most normally athletic young men—that he was much too fat. On Nero, for his part, Agricola probably made no impression at all; he was just one more of the hundreds of place-seekers whom Seneca and Burrus insisted that he ought to see. Nero wished it was evening, when he could slip out of a back door incognito, go to a tavern, and amuse himself, with a gang of young rowdies, beating up respectable citizens in the unlighted streets.

Seneca, on the other hand, would be delighted to see Græcinus' son and to indulge in reminiscences of his father. With Seneca's backing, Agricola's commission would not be long delayed: the Emperor's grant of the Broad Stripe (a four-inch-wide purple border to the white knee-length tunic), which meant that after his army service he could expect senatorial rank.

The desired posting to Britain would take longer. The emperor gave the rank, but the actual appointment of Military Tribune (staff officer in a legion or at an army headquarters), with which a future senator began his career, was in the gift of the army-commander concerned, up to the limit of his establishment—six per legion. The way to get it was by letters of recommendation from the Right People. Seneca or Burrus may have helped again. Their letters, commending Græcinus' son to Suetonius Paulinus, Governor and Commander-in-Chief in Britain, would go by the imperial courier service; but even so, an answer could not be expected in less than several weeks.

At last, however, there arrived a favourable reply from the great man. Yes, there would be a vacancy for the coming year, and Agricola would be welcome. There would be the further excitement of collecting the necessary equipment; and early in the year 61, Gnæus, with the small retinue of servants befitting his rank, rode off on the long journey by the trunk road to Boulogne. One imagines him stopping for a few nights at the family home, and that his mother, kept informed by letters, would be there to receive him and think how well he looked in uniform. Then one morning the cavalcade starts again, the baggage heavier with maternal gifts. Procilla watches them to the bend of the road, and turns back to the house, telling herself that these colonial wars were not really usually very dangerous.

As a matter of fact, he was going to some of the grimmest fighting that a Roman army had seen for over fifty years.

Chapter Three

First Steps in Britain

LEAVING the white cliffs on its left, the transport galley with Agricola and his servants and horses ran on northward, probably for another two or three hours, to reach the sound that then parted the mainland from the Isle of Thanet. Here lay the harbour of Richborough. (Both Roman names—Rutupiæ, Thanatus—are still recognisable.) A long line of entrenchments from sea to sea, protected a vast hutted camp, the main base of the invasion army of eighteen years before; but most of its lines were empty now and growing dilapidated. The chief occupants by now would be the crews of the transport squadron keeping up communications with the continent, and perhaps one or two police and revenue cutters. The Romans still used the Channel ports for the sake of the short sea passage, but heavy goods, whether army stores or merchandise, went on without breaking bulk to the Port of London.

Agricola, one fancies, like a good Roman, preferred to get ashore at once. The transport of horses by ancient ships was something more than inconvenient. He could, of course, as an officer on active service, have used the imperial post facilities, changing horses at the road-houses provided at regular intervals along the main roads. But he would then have had to buy one or more chargers and some pack-horses for his servants and kit on arrival in his province; and it seems more likely that he would bring his own horses from home, rather than run the risk of whatever hard-mouthed and cynical animals he might find at the front.

From Richborough to London by the new Watling Street was about seventy miles. Most travellers broke the journey at Rochester on the Medway, where there was a

27

road-house. London, when reached, proved to be quite a busy place, new, raw and untidy, with a bridge almost on the site of our London Bridge, and trading-vessels tied up to wharves beside a straggling line of wooden warehouses. The Roman customs-house (which certainly existed, for provincial customs revenue was important) must have been on or very near the site of the present one. Agricola may have met in London the finance officer of the province, Decianus Catus, an unpleasant character, but suave at the sight of Agricola's Broad Stripe. The official capital was at Colchester, as in the days of King Cymbeline; there was a Roman colony of retired soldiers there now, and the compulsory purchase, or worse, by which the land for it had been acquired had given rise to more bitterness than any Roman yet realised. But the finance officer, if not at London, was probably up-country among the Iceni, where King Prasutagus had died and Rome had decided to annex. In any case, Agricola's duties lay with the army in the north-west; so—assuming, as seems likeliest, that Paulinus was already at his advanced headquarters planning the summer's campaign—Agricola will have left London after a night or two, travelling with the next mounted party going "up the line". The straight new Roman road ran west across open fields on the line of Oxford Street; forked half-right from the Great West Road on the site of Marble Arch; and plunged forthwith into the virgin forests along the Edgware Road.

So this was Britain: dank, primitive and untamed, outside of the broad swathe of forest felled on each side of the road as a precaution against ambushes. The general wetness and the frequently grey skies contributed to make the picture most unattractive to a soldier from the Mediterranean. "The weather is filthy, with frequent rain and fog," says Tacitus; his informant is certainly Agricola, and there is little doubt that some such comment figured also in Agricola's first letters home. Twenty miles out from London, where the forest gave place to chalk hills, there was a market town, Verulamium (now St. Albans), with a few new Roman-style buildings; but after that there was not a sign of civilisation. Dense belts of forest, a day's

FIRST STEPS IN BRITAIN

march wide, alternated with bare uplands; the heavy clay
soils of the midlands were still almost uninhabited. The
nights were spent in bleak rest-houses at the stockaded
posting-stations; it was all very different from what a
hundred years of Roman occupation had made of the road
across Gaul. Among the names in the official *Route*, of
which Agricola may have had a copy, one stood out as
familiar: Mediolanum, far up near the front; "Mid Vale"
in Celtic. It was the name of a great town in Gallic North
Italy, now Milan. But when seen later it proved to be
nothing but another group of huts, at a road-fork in the
Cheshire plain.

At Venonæ—High Cross, on the borders of Warwick and
Leicestershire—the party emerged from dense forest once
more, and crossed the Fosse Way, the great road from Lincoln to Exeter, laid out by Ostorius to give lateral communication and to demarcate the limits of the pacified
area. This was over half-way from London to Viroconium
on the Severn, the base-camp of the central army. To
Viroconium the road continued, via Letocetum, Penno-
crucium, Uxacona—names which have left traces in the
first halves of the modern Lichfield, Penkridge and Oaken-
gates; and at Wroxeter, under the Wrekin, Agricola
probably joined his unit and reported to Paulinus.

The position of the frontier in Britain had altered little
in the nine summers since the capture of Caradoc. Even
without him the indomitable Silures had proved quite able
to look after themselves. The First Silurian War, it is not
always realised, ended in defeat for the Romans. By fierce,
sudden attacks on working-parties and convoys, the Silures
inflicted heavy losses and entirely foiled the Roman attempt to establish forward posts in their mountains. Once
they even defeated a legion in the field. Ostorius died
in harness, worn out by his efforts; and under his
successor, Didius, distinguished but elderly, the war lan-
guished.

Didius was also distracted by trouble among the
Brigantes, where the pro-Roman court faction split on a
private issue. Queen Cartimandua, tiring of her consort

Venutius, divorced him and married a younger man, his
armour-bearer; and Venutius, thus converted, it appears,
to the view that a woman's rule was a bad thing, gained
the backing of the anti-foreign warriors. Civil war started.
Cartimandua contrived to entrap Venutius' brother and
some of his kinsmen; but if she hoped to stop Venutius by
using them as hostages, the attempt failed. Soon Venutius
with an army of tribesmen was threatening her capital.
Didius sent to her aid some of his auxiliary cohorts—Gallic
or German light infantry battalions; but they ran into
heavy opposition and made little headway. Didius had to
reinforce with a whole legion—probably the IXth; and
even this powerful unit only gained a victory after surviving some awkward moments. Venutius was a renowned
tactician. At last, however, he admitted defeat and retired
northwards. A place named Venutio (perhaps for Castellum
Venutii, Venutius' Castle), one march from Newstead on
the Tweed, may possibly represent a fort where he lurked
awhile among the Selgovæ of Selkirk; and now that archæology has revealed traces of pre-Agricolan Roman camps
in Dumfriesshire, it has been suggested that Cæsius Nasica,
who was in charge of these operations, may have penetrated
beyond the Border in pursuit of him. The alliance with
Cartimandua remained a bastion of Roman policy in
Britain; but it was beginning to be a bastion that needed
propping up.

The next governor of Britain died within a year of his
arrival; and thus it was that on the arrival of Paulinus,
about 59, the Roman lines still stood very much where
they had stood under Ostorius. Nero, with his love of
dramatic gestures, had, it is said, even thought of abandon-
ing Britain altogether; the province certainly cannot have
been able to pay for its garrison at this time. However, he
had been over-persuaded, and the new governor was a great
soldier and an expert in mountain warfare. Many years
before, he had led the first Roman column to cross the
Atlas Mountains, during a "little war" in Morocco. His
first step was to reach the Irish Sea near Chester, cutting
off Wales from the north; a move which Ostorius had been
carrying out ten years before when recalled by trouble on

his flanks. At the moment when Agricola reported to him, he was planning a great blow at the enemy's morale and his economic resources; an attack on the Druid stronghold and fertile cornlands of Mona, the Isle of Anglesey.

Agricola plunged at once into the task of learning all he could about Britain and about the army. It was the natural and sensible thing to do, since for a young Roman of the governing class, who might some day be a general, this early military service offered the best opportunity of "learning the trade". Many young noblemen appear to have taken their work extremely lightly, no doubt assuming that what their fathers and grandfathers had done they could do when the time came. They would give the orders and ("Carry on, sergeant-major!") their veteran centurions would see them carried out. But not so the young man from Forum Julii.

He knew, of course, the main facts about army organisation: six "centuries", each of eighty men in practice, under a centurion, made one cohort; ten cohorts, one legion. That was the sort of thing that a Roman boy could not remember *not* knowing. But as the army was constantly changing and evolving, there would always be some surprises. In any case, there was much in the working of such a complex mechanism that one could never learn except by seeing it in action.

Each legion had, as its general, usually a senator in his thirties, changing every three or four years. He was called, like more senior generals, the Legate, a word literally meaning "deputy", i.e. deputy of the Emperor as generalissimo. The Legate of a Legion had as staff officers six Tribunes, a title dating from the time when the Legion meant the levy of the three Tribes of primitive Rome. Most of these were "knights"; about one per legion was a future senator. Each century had a deputy-centurion called the *Optio*, a company standard-bearer, a corporal of the watch, who kept the ticket on which the password of the day was written, and a group of senior soldiers who received extra pay and were excused fatigues.

The first cohort in each legion under the empire was of double size, but had only five "centuries", really of much greater strength. Their *optiones* were naturally very important. This left one centurion (out of an establishment of sixty) to spare; and he was, it appears, the headquarters centurion, an exceedingly important person, who supervised much of the discipline and administration, attended councils of war with the tribunes and Legate, and in battle took charge of the silver eagle which was the standard of the legion. To the first cohort belonged, it seems likely, such special details as clerks and orderlies; the artillerymen for the great catapults, that could be used effectively in the field as well as in, or against, fortified positions; perhaps also a medical section, though some lowlier "doctors"—medical orderlies, with a training in first-aid—were distributed, like the armourer-smiths, among all companies. All specialists were soldiers, and took their place in the line of battle; and every legionary who was not a specialist was either a joiner or a mason or, at the very least, a skilled pioneer.

Much routine work, which we should associate with the quartermaster-general's branch, was taken off the shoulders of the Legate and his staff by the camp-prefect or camp-commandant, often loosely called the Prefect of the Legion; a promoted senior centurion, ending his active career in this position and usually making a fortune out of it. Centurions, socially speaking, were a mixed lot. Many had risen from the ranks; but some also were commissioned straight into the rank of centurion; they were usually sons of leading families from small towns, sometimes even minor members of the equestrian class, and it was probably from among these educated men that the leading centurions were usually recruited. If they reached the leading positions young enough, they might then be promoted into the equestrian grade as officers of the Guard cohorts at Rome.

Each legion had also 120 mounted men, but they seem to have been used merely as orderlies, etc. For cavalry, the empire relied on regiments raised among the horse-riding peoples of lands outside the rugged Mediterranean area; Gauls, Spaniards and Pannonians (from western Hungary) formed the bulk of the mounted regiments or "Wings" in Britain, while some British cavalry gained a high reputation in central Europe. Such "allies" (the normal word used for non-citizen subjects of the empire) also supplied the light-armed infantry cohorts, of 480 or 960 men, never brigaded into legions, which held the outpost forts on the frontiers, and skirmished ahead of the legions during campaigns. Some of these cohorts, of both sizes, had twenty-five per cent. mounted men, a convenient arrangement for minor frontier operations at battalion strength.

With the passage of time, all these "auxiliary" units tended to evolve from tribal levies, like the Gallic and German cavalry which Cæsar had used in Gaul, into Roman regular troops, gaining in discipline, but losing something of the qualities that had originally made them so useful as scouts and in guerilla operations; and the Romans in turn continually raised limited numbers of new barbarian levies, valued precisely for their barbarian fighting qualities, and as being cheap and expendable. During Agricola's time, the most recently acquired barbarian "allies" were friendly Britons. In A.D. 80 some were being discharged on the continent, and granted Roman citizenship as part of the usual reward after twenty-five years' service; that is, since so early as the year 55. Agricola himself employed others against the Caledonians; and it is therefore likely, though evidence is lacking, that such "friendlies" were also being used on the Welsh marches in the fifties and sixties. A recruiting ground lay ready to hand, among the Cornovii of Shropshire and Cheshire and the Dobunni of the Cotswolds, natural enemies both of the invading Belgæ and of the Welsh mountain tribes. These people seem to have submitted easily to Rome's blandishments. They prospered as a result. As Richmond has pointed out, their Romanised capitals—Wroxeter, Cirencester—contrast notably, by their size, with the small capitals of those peoples which, like the Silures, fought fiercely against the Romans and paid the penalty.

It was among these peoples, then, that Agricola formed first impressions of the Britons which, through many vicissitudes, were to endure. Good, vigorous fellows, he thought; *impigri*—an expressive Roman word. In Tacitus' account of the British character, one seems to hear the voice of Agricola, the retired general, twenty-five years later: "They put up with conscription, taxation and other burdens of the empire with a will, if they are not treated unfairly. If they are, they become very difficult. Conquest has made them obedient, but not servile, so far."

Agricola's exemplary keenness won the approval of Suetonius, who would in any case have been watching him, since he was a Broad Stripe tribune. Within a few weeks the governor picked him out of his legion to be his personal assistant and messmate, who would share his tent on the forthcoming campaign. He may not yet have shared with an untried staff officer the great secret of just where he was proposing to strike; but one of the major preparatory works now nearing completion was the building of some fast galleys and a large flotilla of flat-bottomed boats, probably on the Cheshire Dee.

As soon as the spring weather was judged favourable enough, the army moved out, on the road northwards, away from the Silures, who doubtless noted their going with relief not unmixed with mystification; but they still had the Second Legion at Gloucester to keep an eye on. At the road-fork of Mediolanum the column turned north-west. Presently the Roman road ended abruptly, and the troops stumbled on, on rough tracks, western European cavalry and light infantry scouting ahead and on the flanks, legionaries farther in, sweating under their armour, weapons, palisade-stakes, entrenching tools and several days' meal for making bread or porridge. A long string of pack-animals used the main track, carrying reserve food, heavy equipment and the leather ridge-tents, called pavilions or "butterflies", because that was what they looked like when spread out on the ground. Every night the army dug in; with the 20,000 stakes carried by two legions firmly planted in the upcast from a ditch, beaten down hard, an army of 20,000 horse and foot could be protected very effectively. Ten or twelve miles a day would be good going on an advance into enemy country. The commander-in-chief and his staff would be well up, using the main track (if any), ahead of the baggage. And so, from some hill in Wales, Agricola caught his first sight of the sea beyond Britain.

The army pushed on, keeping near the coast, brushing aside whatever harassing opposition the Ordovices could offer. They crossed a river called in Celtic the Var (now the Clwyd); Agricola remembered another Var in Provence, half-way between his father's property at Fréjus and his mother's at Ventimiglia. Suetonius probably bridged it and left a cohort to guard the crossing. There was a Roman post there later for centuries, known as Castellum Varæ, "Castle Var", or Varæ for short. A few days later, advance-guards were over the Conway, a river whose name has scarcely changed; the Roman fort at this crossing was called Kanovium. The mountains of Snowdonia rose darkly ahead; but the Ordovices, their inhabitants, were faced with some awkward guessing. They would naturally have removed their women, children and flocks to places of relative safety; but which way were the invaders going to push next? South, up the Conway, for instance, or west, down the Carnarvon peninsula? Most of the warriors, one can be quite sure, insisted on staying to look after their homes in Merioneth and Denbighshire. It was not till the Roman main army marched over the hills west of Conway that the chiefs could even try with any hope of success to move men from the south flank; and not until the arrival of the flotilla, which it would be reasonable for Suetonius to hold back till the last moment, that they could be sure that the holy isle of Mona itself was menaced.

What the Anglesey men alone could do, they did. They manned the shore of the Mona (or Menai) Straits; and the Druids of the groves of Mona, not neglecting the spiritual arm, assembled to call down the wrath of heaven upon the invaders if they touched that shore. Since the days of the Megalithic dolmen-builders, Mona had been a stronghold of the western sea-folk and their religion; Druids from Gaul, Cæsar tells us, used to go to Britain to study; and from Britain, since the Roman invasion, many irreconcilables had fled to Anglesey. In its latest or Celtic phase (we know nothing of its earlier character) the western religion was a barbarous and cruel affair; omens were drawn from the twitching limbs of a victim stabbed in the back, and human sacrifice was common and deemed essential. Whatever one may think of the ethics of the Roman conquest, it was an evil thing that they were now marching to destroy.

At low tide, for the sake especially of the cavalry who would have to swim their horses, the assault was launched. Eight Batavian cohorts from the mouths of the Rhine, for whom water obstacles had no terrors, formed a part of the army—probably its first wave. As the invaders approached, they saw the shore facing them held by a motley throng. Among and between the bands of warriors, women in ceremonial black, with hair streaming on their shoulders, rushed from place to place brandishing torches in the air. "Like Furies in a Greek play," thought Agricola. Behind them could be seen the fires of sacrifice and the grim figures of the Druids, with hands upraised, calling down the curse that should paralyse the enemy and make him stand motionless to be cut down by British arms. Many of the Roman soldiers, themselves scarcely emancipated from this sort of thing, actually were, for the moment, not a little shaken; but their officers urged them not to be panic-stricken before a horde of priests and women; the men took up the cry, not so much in .a spirit of rationalist scepticism as in the faith that Rome's magic was stronger; the spell was broken, and with cheering and rivalry legions and auxiliaries thrust the flat-bottomed boats across the narrows at the best speed of oars and quant-poles. The cavalry followed, picking their way through the shallows and swimming when necessary. Two legions, 4,000 Batavians, other light infantry and cavalry, made short work of the Ordovices and exiles drawn up on the beach; and many Druids, standing their ground with the courage of fanaticism, were cut down where they stood or thrust into their own altar fires.

Then the whole island was overrun and thoroughly pillaged. A great hoard of Early Iron Age metal-work, found during World War II in the now drained pool of Llyn Cerrig Bach may, some have thought, have been pitched in by the victors; though it is perhaps more likely that it

represents spoils of war and other offerings cast cere-
monially into a sacred lake by the Britons. There were
spear-heads, swords and their scabbards, shield-mountings,
chariot-fittings, part of a bronze trumpet, iron currency-
bars such as Cæsar mentions, and gang-chains for slaves.
The bloodstained groves where so many human victims
had suffered were razed to the ground; and Suetonius prepared to garrison Mona and to take a shaken Wales in the
rear.

While he was still engaged in this, a panting messenger
on a lathered horse brought him a message, probably from
the finance officer, Decianus. The Iceni had risen with
fury against the proposed annexation, and were calling
upon all tribes to join them. They were quite out of hand;
the small forces in the south-east were powerless. The
presence of the commander-in-chief with the main army
was urgently wanted. In the meantime, Decianus was doing
what he could for the defence of Colchester.

There was nothing for it but to call in outlying detachments and return by forced marches by the way they had
come.

Chapter Four

Fire and the Sword

TO give the necessary orders was an easy matter. Transmitting them involved plenty of work for a keen young officer. As usual, to decide what it was desirable to do was the least part of a general's task; the labour was in getting it done, especially with an army spread out between Lincoln, Holyhead and Gloucester, and with the speed of even the most vital message limited to that of a galloping horse.

The Ordovices would have to wait. The whole army must come back at least to the Dee. After that, it would be necessary to leave a skeleton force facing the mountain tribes, while the main army dealt with the Iceni. Venonæ, at the intersection of the Fosse Way and Watling Street, would be a natural meeting-place. This was assuming that Decianus' messages were not the product of mere panic; but the facts certainly sounded serious enough. That the annexation of the Iceni had run into trouble was unexpected, but not perhaps very surprising; but the fury with which the Britons rose astonished everybody. Agricola realised only later and gradually how bad the provocation had been.

To begin with, there were many widespread grievances. The ex-soldier colonists, established at Colchester, had not been content with the land allotted them once and for all, but were continuing to take in more. If they troubled even to allege any legal pretext, Tacitus does not mention it. Britons were conquered people, they said; therefore they were slaves, and their property was their masters'. The governor was far away, and busy with military matters; and armed force on the spot was represented by a detachment of probably elderly troops, who were the less disposed to interfere since they hoped to increase the provision made for their own old age in the same way. Again, Claudius had apparently made grants to many British notables towards the expenses of Romanising their way of life. The Britons had believed these to be gifts, but Nero's government now insisted that they were loans, and Decianus demanded repayment. This, especially in view of Nero's flirtation with the idea of evacuation, was quite enough to cause other money-lenders to call in their loans; foremost among them no less a personage than Seneca.

Seneca, having grown fantastically rich since he became the Emperor's chief minister, had been prominent among those who saw in the new province a field for the investment of their surplus wealth, and had used the government's influence to thrust his loans even upon unwilling borrowers. The idea, presumably, was that the loans should be used for developing the country, producing a surplus which would yield taxes for the treasury and interest for Seneca. But British chiefs and landholders, thus entangled in a cash nexus which was entirely mysterious to them, proved disappointing clients; and with the treasury now recalling its grants, Seneca, nervous about his money, decided to do the same thing in his private capacity. His agents in Britain thus had the opportunity to show how quick they could be in clamping down on a debtor. Government procurators, too, from the Finance Officer downwards, would gladly do anything to help the chief minister; and smaller money-lenders had an opportunity to produce, at a price, the ready money required by the victims of Seneca's transaction. There was thus widespread impoverishment in Britain, and a widespread feeling of desperation—a feeling that whether one fought or no, Rome meant to squeeze and suck the life-blood out of her new province—even before the treatment of Boudicca, Queen of the Iceni, supplied the spark that set the whole land on fire.

Prasutagus, King of the Iceni and one of the richest men in Britain, had no son to succeed him. In any case, Rome's treaties with client kings were always made with individuals, and might be renewed, or not, at pleasure when the crown demised. Foreseeing the inevitable, Prasutagus by his will made the Emperor co-heir with his wife and daughters, hoping in this way to secure at least an orderly annexation; but it was a vain hope, with the administration of the south-east in its then condition. Decianus with a troop of soldiers and slave members of his financial staff, all equally out for loot, invaded his kingdom, seizing private estates indiscriminately, and proceeded to take possession of his house. There was probably a scuffle; for Boudicca, described as a tall, blonde, deep-voiced, masterful woman, was not of a type to submit tamely to injustice. The Romans were thereby simply provoked to do their worst. The house was sacked, as though taken by storm; the two girls were raped and Boudicca herself whipped like a refractory slave.

The Iceni were thus shown quite clearly what to expect as soon as the Romans were really in the saddle, and also provided, in the person of their outraged queen, at once with a symbol and with a commander, who, if no strategist, proved a fierce and vigorous war-leader. They rose as one man, with arms improvised or manufactured or hidden since the days of Ostorius; and the finance officer and his minions were soon running for their lives. The bestiality of these Romans' behaviour had been, indeed, only equalled by its madness, for the forces at hand were far too few to cope with any serious trouble. Frantic messages were sent off to Suetonius in Wales and to Petillius Cerialis, Legate of the IXth at Lincoln; while the colonists at Colchester in their turn appealed to Decianus, on his reappearance, to reinforce their meagre garrison.

Decianus, combing out his taxation and excise offices, sent along some two hundred police and orderlies with a scratch collection of arms; and for some days life at Camulodunum proceeded in an uneasy calm. The Trinovantes, so far, were unaffected; and once the legions came, they would soon suppress the trouble among the Iceni. Chiefs of the Trinovantes, of long-standing loyalty—even priests of the late deified Emperor Claudius—assured their Roman friends that they could answer for their people. In secret, many of them were in touch with the Iceni. The

rising had sent a thrill through Britain. Also the chiefs of
the Trinovantes had found their priesthoods a most expensive honour, and were beginning to feel that this was
just one more way of getting the Britons parted from their
property. However, on their assurance, no entrenchments
were dug, and a proposal to evacuate the women and children was not carried out.

Suetonius, back on the Dee, left the bulk of XX Legion
under its commander, with some auxiliary battalions, to
put up a bold front against the unconquered tribes and to
prevent the Welsh and the Brigantes from getting together.
The XIVth, with a detachment of the XXth (probably a
third of its strength), continued down Watling Street.
"And as for us," one fancies Suetonius saying to Agricola,
"we are going to London."

The parting of the two legions in Cheshire, as it turned
out, was to determine and sever their fates for ever. For
the XIVth, the march south-east was to bring danger, victory, glory, many changes of station, and a chequered
career as far as the Rhine, the Danube and the Po. For
the XXth, the north-west frontier was to be for some three
centuries a permanent home.

Riding fast with a few squadrons of cavalry, Suetonius
and Agricola soon left the infantry column out of sight.
They would meet, all the more quickly, the messages from
the south-east coming "up the line". All the news was bad.
The rising was spreading, and presently the trickle of
messages dried up altogether. The road was cut by
guerillas north-west of London, and the despatch-riders
(not soldiers, but civil-service slaves of "Cæsar's Household") had fled for the coast or for the nearest forts. Somewhere on Watling Street Agricola will have passed his
twenty-first birthday—13th June. He must have wondered
what the chances were of his seeing his twenty-second.

News from the other divisions of the army was unsatisfactory too. The IInd at Gloucester was, most unfortunately, without its regular commander; and its camp-
commandant, Pœnius Postumus, an elderly officer, made
no move to leave his cantonments. Probably he argued that

41

it was impossible to withdraw troops from the Silurian front without risking invasion from that side too. Paulinus could do nothing but send him, from Watling Street, furious messages reiterating the order.

Cerialis, commanding the IXth, on the other hand, was a gallant and impetuous soldier, whom Agricola was to know and admire in Britain in later years; and he, naturally hearing of the revolt long before Paulinus, marched, on his own initiative, by the direct road south.

This was all very fine, but he was not there to meet Suetonius in the midlands. Once or more, no doubt, there were messages from him to say what troops he was taking and to describe his movements and intentions. Then, as both he and Paulinus drew nearer to the enemy, the fog of war enveloped them and there was no more news at all.

"Through the midst of the enemy," says Tacitus, "Suetonius, undaunted, made his way to London." Agricola was not likely to forget that ride: the burnt-out post-stations, the occasional corpse in the road, the marauders scuttling away into the forest at the sight of the cavalry. There was no sign yet of the enemy's main forces. (They had, in fact, gone to meet Cerialis.) At Verulamium, the traders and their families came out to cheer the party and the news that the legions were following; but the only news from the east was all vague rumour of Roman disasters and the sack of settlements.

Next day they reached London. To secure and defend this important centre was Suetonius' intention. But here definite news met him of the triumph of the insurgents. Colchester had fallen and thousands of Romans had been massacred. Lulled by the soft words of "friendly" natives, they had been slack in their arrangements to defend themselves; and then the Trinovantes had risen, "friendlies" and all. Anti-Roman secret societies, it transpired later, had existed for years. The colonists were caught dispersed about their daily tasks "as though in peace-time", and overwhelmed by a horde of enemies. The few hundred troops occupied the new Temple of Claudius, whose solid plinth still exists under Colchester Castle, and held out for two days; then the Britons swept over them, and there was an end of them too.

Worse still, from a military point of view, there was sinister confirmation of reports concerning a disaster to the IXth. No message got through from Cerialis, but Paulinus became convinced that there was "sufficient evidence". Probably enemy bands had been displaying captured standards—a regular trick of ancient psychological warfare. It was true; somewhere in the eastern counties the IXth had run into the enemy in overwhelming numbers, had been outflanked and not merely driven back but destroyed as a formation. Some cut their way out, including Cerialis and his mounted men; but two thousand Roman legionaries fell on the field, while Cerialis with the cavalry retreated to Lincoln and put the defence of the base in order. Here he was unmolested; for Boudicca, with her Iceni reinforced by a horde of Catuvellauni and Trinovantes, had turned southward again to march upon London.

Paulinus came to the terrible decision that London must be evacuated. The IInd Legion, if they had moved promptly, might have got there in time; but the legion-and-a-bit from North Wales were still days behind and, with only his escort and civilians, to defend the long, straggling, unwalled town would be hopeless. He must rejoin and take command of the little army in the midlands, on which now depended the only hope of saving anything. One wonders indeed why the Britons had not cut through between Paulinus and his troops, or, earlier, between Paulinus and London, as they could easily have done by way of the chalk ridge, the ancient Icknield Way. The reason no doubt is that they were not an organised army, but a popular rising. With no systematic intelligence, they probably neither knew nor cared where the governor was, having little conception of how much difference his resolute but prudent leadership might yet make. Also they let themselves be delayed by the intervention of Cerialis and his devoted column; and they lost more time by stopping, both at Colchester and elsewhere, to torture any Romans, men, women or children, whom they caught.

There was horror and dismay among the population of London; but Suetonius was adamant. For him to stay would not save them. Civilians, he announced, might accompany his force, if they could, to the only existing shelter—the Roman army. There is no suggestion that they could retire south of the Thames; presumably the south country was in rebellion too; nor yet that anyone could or did hide in the woods. London and Verulam were already like islets in a hostile sea, awaiting the great tidal wave of Boudicca's army. As for the ships in the river, they could take only a fraction of the populace. Probably they had already gone. On one of them, getting out with a whole skin, characteristically of his kind, had gone Decianus Catus, who had done as much to cause the rising as any one man.

With none too much start, it appears, the retreat began; a pitiful stream of civilians of every age and both sexes, convoyed by Paulinus' cavalry, so long as they could keep up. All who stayed or who fell behind were done to death by the Britons, transformed into fiends by eighteen years of what had, at least latterly, been extreme misgovernment and oppression.

As they straggled along the north-western road, not far out of London, a frightful horde was pouring down upon it, from the north or north-east: warriors of the Iceni and field-slaves loosed from their fetters, captured Roman standards, heads on poles and remains of Early Iron Age pageantry; Boudicca herself, high on her chariot, with her yellow hair falling to her waist and her harsh voice exchanging pleasantries with the chieftains about her. The wooden houses of London went up in flames. Civilians who had not fled might offer ransom if they were brought safe to the continent; but, says Tacitus, the insurgents seemed less keen on gain than to butcher, impale, burn and crucify, as though sure that punishment would overtake them and determined to snatch their revenge while they could.

In the crypt of the Church of All Hallows by the Tower (under repair at the time of writing, after damage suffered in a later war) can be seen a section of red-brick wall which stood above ground in the London of the later Roman period; and below that a hard, black layer about an inch thick. It is a layer of ash, hard pressed and compact by the weight of the buildings resting upon it through the centuries: the ashes of the fire in which Boudicca burnt London in the year 61.

Already weary, the refugees hobbled into Verulam. There would be food there, and perhaps a night's rest under roofs. Another unhappy contingent joined the column, or perhaps had already been warned to go ahead. Afterwards, nights of terror and misery on the damp ground alternated with days of footsore marching, urged on by the escorting cavalry and the fear of death. Behind them, Verulam burned and the horrors of Colchester and London were re-enacted. Seventy thousand Romans and Roman subjects are said (probably with great exaggeration) to have perished in the three towns. There had been no such massacre of Romans since the Greeks of Asia were given their revenge by King Mithradates, 150 years before.

Perhaps three or four days out of London, the refugees met the army. Safety at last! But it was a perilously small army; barely 10,000 men even now. There was still no sign of the IInd; and in view of the supply situation, it would soon be urgently necessary to fight without them.

But Suetonius did not halt the retreat until he reached a place—probably noted at some earlier passing—suitable for giving battle. After an open plain, dense forest began abruptly, and the road ran into it across a salient of open ground. There was observation over the ground across which Boudicca's army, now in hot pursuit, would come; and the forest was so dense that no significant numbers of enemy could infiltrate to get at his rear.

This description, it does not seem to have been noticed before, enables us to identify approximately the site of the battle, on which Tacitus, as usual, says nothing. Suetonius' army returning from Wales would certainly be moving along Watling Street; and the battlefield was at a point where, coming from London, the road suddenly passed from open country into forest. Very little artificial clearing of the forest had been done in pre-Roman times. The wide open space to the south-east was therefore a *natural* open space, with a soil on which forest trees do not naturally grow; and the edge of the now vanished forest should be represented by the south-eastern edge of a belt of dense clay soil. One place where the road comes on to such soil is near Fenny Stratford, after leaving the chalk and the cretaceous sandstone country; but the clay here is low-lying, and a force standing before the edge of the clay-forest would have neither the advantage of position nor (what Tacitus seems to imply) clear observation to the south-east. A likelier spot therefore seems to be north-west of Towcester, at the edge of the Jurassic clay, near where the headwaters of the Nene emerge from the Northamptonshire uplands. For the benefit of modern travellers it may be added that the railway from London to Rugby, north of Weedon station, here almost follows the Roman road. Not far north-east are the fields of two other small but decisive battles: Bosworth and Naseby. The cause which led to all three being fought on these midland ridges is the same as that which determined the siting of the Watling Street and Fosse Way: it is the fact that through this area must pass any army which is to march across central England without crossing any considerable river.

Paulinus would willingly have retreated farther; but his supply position was becoming alarming, and unless he could win a victory he could not forage. However, once his flanks were safe, he seems to have felt there was ground for confidence that his veterans could dispose of any number of Britons, especially their present undisciplined hordes. He rode along the ranks telling the troops so, and pointing out that even in engagements between armies of equal size it was usually only a small proportion of the combatants who ever really struck a blow at the enemy. He even used that already venerable cliché of the outnumbered general: "We few—we happy few. . . ." His object in choosing this narrow-fronted position was to force the Britons to bunch, so that he could massacre them. In an open plain they could spread out and engulf him, without offering any central mass at which he could strike.

Here he could get the "outside station" and strike inwards at a jammed enemy. His cavalry, supported by light infantry, were on the wings as usual, and his instructions to their officers were, at the given signal, to charge and then turn inward. Some enemy would be left between the cavalry wings and the legionary centre, but that could not be helped; anyhow, most of them would be too dismayed to think of exploiting their position. He had not enough troops to form a continuous line that could envelop the enemy; but after the javelins of the legionaries had taken toll of their advance, it should be possible to attack in three separate compact bodies, with the enemy no longer in a condition to take advantage of their separation. So much we can infer by comparing Tacitus with the later historian Dio, who, though his actual battle-piece is rhetorical nonsense, gives some interesting evidence on Suetonius' formation and tactics, as well as, earlier, on the causes and course of the revolt.

The Britons came on in enormous numbers, filling the road for miles, and deploying into dense disorderly masses before the Roman position. Behind them came into sight a huge wagon-train, bearing their supplies, but also great numbers of their women-folk, who would look after the beasts while the men were fighting, and would also enjoy the spectacle of the crowning victory. These also spread out gradually into a great straggling wagon-park behind the warriors, at a point where a ridge or a detached belt of forest cut off the view. Chiefs in their Homeric chariots stood out above the masses, and Boudicca herself with her daughters could clearly be seen, riding along the front and shouting to her warriors to slaughter these fugitives and to avenge their wrongs and hers. Suetonius utilised the interval further to encourage his own troops; he professed to discern more women than men in the host opposite. The men cheered him, swinging their brawny javelin-arms; it was with confidence of the outcome that the general rode back to take up his position in the centre of the line.

Now the Britons began to come forward, yelling and waving their weapons, crowding more densely still into the

47

angle between the woods as the foremost of them waited for their rear to close up. Agricola, sitting his horse next to Suetonius, steals, one fancies, a sidelong glance at him; but the grim face of the Governor gave no sign. It suited him well that his men should have a packed target for the deadly javelins that prepared the way for a Roman charge. Every legionary carried two of these: the light *pilum* for a longer and the heavy for a shorter range. Their line was drawn up in loose order; when the front rank had thrown the slighter *pilum*, the second rank came through the intervals and did likewise; then the third; and then, if the array was a deep one, all three lines of a second cohort might pass through those of the front line and throw theirs. After that, with the precision given by years of drill, the whole process was repeated at close range with the heavier *pilum*.

Suetonius waited till the Britons were dense and close before him and their attack was imminent. Then he signalled. In about the next thirty seconds ten thousand javelins smashed into the crowded and unarmoured ranks; and then, with their short heavy swords, and in a wedge formation—the exposed flanks held back—the legionaries hurled themselves upon the already shaken enemy. Simultaneously on both wings lances came down to the level and the cavalry charged. Ill-led and at a terrible disadvantage in equipment, the Britons went down in hundreds. Their very numbers gave the Romans hard work for a time; but before long all but the bravest were thinking of flight, and the bravest were dead. Then there was a still more fearful carnage at the wagon-lines; for the wagons acted as an obstacle to those trying to escape, and the first Romans to get to them killed the draft-animals. Men, women and beasts lay in one frightful shambles. Roman rumour claimed cheerfully that 230,000 Britons were engaged and 80,000 killed. Of the Romans, 400 were killed and slightly more wounded—in all, just under ten per cent. casualties. The XIVth Legion had covered itself with glory, and was rewarded with two new titles of honour. Known hitherto as Gemina, the "Double Legion" (formed out of two depleted formations during the Civil Wars), it appears hereafter as Gemina Martia Victrix, "The Martial, the Victorious": as we might say, the Fighting Fourteenth.

Boudicca escaped and reached her own country; but she was a broken woman. Whether by poison, as Tacitus says, or by sickness, as Dio, she died soon after, to be given a royal funeral—the funeral, men must have felt, of the Icenian kingdom—by her doomed countrymen.

At Gloucester, Pœnius Postumus heard of the battle with mixed feelings. He had been wrong every way: wrong in law—he had disobeyed orders; wrong in his appreciation of what could be done—his legion might have saved London and many thousands of lives; wrong to lose his nerve; Paulinus had dared, and won. He drew out his sword, set the point between his ribs and drove it home.

The war was won, but not over. Suetonius called in units from all sides—even the IInd came now; and over 10,000 fresh troops, including 2,000 legionaries to recruit the shattered IXth, were sent from the continent. The land of the Iceni was invaded and devastated—a bronze head of Claudius, found in the River Alde in Suffolk, was probably loot cast away at this time—and the other tribes which had joined in or even in any way behaved unsatisfactorily during the rebellion shared in their punishment. There was horrible devastation, and also famine; for the rebellion had broken out in the spring, and the insurgents, rushing to arms, had neglected their fields. Their leaders had comforted them with the thought that for the next year they could live on the corn stored for the Roman army. But so merciless was Suetonius and so savage his troops (some of them had seen the impaled and mutilated bodies of the Roman women) that many guerilla bands still remained at large, the uttermost hardships seeming better than surrender; and presently the new Finance Officer, Julius Classicianus, having in vain appealed for clemency, reported to Rome that while Suetonius was in command he could see no end.

Circles near Suetonius (in which we must clearly include the young Agricola) regarded Classicianus' appeals as weakness and his report as an unworthy piece of inter-departmental rivalry. They even accused him of privily encouraging the rebels to remain in the field and wait for a new governor. It is easier for us to take a wider view; and from a distance it is obvious that he was right.

We know, as it happens, something of Classicianus' background. He was, almost certainly, a Celt, and a northern Celt. His wife, Pacata, was a daughter of Julius Indus, a great man among the Treveri, round Trier in the Rhineland, who had once nipped in the bud a rebellion of his tribe, led by a personal rival. He may well have named his daughter Pacata, "Pacified", in memory of this. He also commanded a famous cavalry regiment, Indus' Horse, which served in the early days in Britain. Classicianus' own "middle name" was Alpinius; and that also was a name of a prominent family in the same tribe. (All prominent families there would be Julii.) Classicianus was thus, like Agricola himself in his later and mellower days, an example of the new type of Roman official, with wider than merely Roman sympathies. He died in London, where his wife, naming herself proudly "Julia Pacata, daughter of Indus", set up a monument to him. It is in the British Museum, and deserves to be known as that of a man who served Britain well.

Nero's government sent over a commission of enquiry, under one of his Greek freedman secretaries—another insult to his general, thought the indignant Agricola. The Greek agreed with the Gaul; and not long after, Suetonius was recalled, on the pretext of having lost some ships of his fleet, probably on the east coast. Agricola went with him, or about that time, still thinking the government very unjust to his general. Britain had peace for ten years; but the small size of the later Romanised capital of the Iceni bears eloquent witness to the depopulation that their rebellion had cost.

Agricola's mother no doubt thought he looked older. She might well.

Chapter Five

Life under Nero (A.D. 62—68)

BACK in Rome, Agricola next served his twelve-months' apprenticeship to administrative or judicial work in the capital.[1] Twenty young future senators every year served this apprenticeship: three in the mint (this was considered the best post, and was often followed by quick promotion); four in charge of repair and maintenance of the streets of Rome; three in the macabre post of supervisors of executions (it would not bother a Roman); and ten as junior judicial officials. The work was not crushing, and there was plenty of time for social life such as would come the way of an agreeable young administrative official, who was also Græcinus' son and had the prestige, in an age which held its wars at decent intervals and at a safe distance, of a returned hero from Britain. Agricola, indeed, certainly was paying much attention to his private affairs during this year; before the summer was over he was married. Julia Procilla doubtless came to Rome for the wedding. After it, like a perfect mother-in-law, she retired to live her own life at her home at Ventimiglia.

Roman marriages were often a matter of family arrangement; especially first marriages, which were by no means always the last. But love-matches were not unknown, and both they and the family-arrangement type often settled down to devoted and lifelong partnerships. Naturally one hears most in literature about those which broke up with the most éclat; but thousands of tombstones of the Roman empire, of folk great or obscure, tell a different story. Agri-

[1] In a later generation this would have been done before his military service, but under the early empire the order varied; and this is perhaps the point at which this post, not mentioned by Tacitus, fits best into his narrative.

cola's marriage was one of the happy ones.

At twenty-two, he was marrying earlier than many Romans. Thirty was quite a common age. His bride, by the custom of the time, was probably not much over fourteen. Her name was Domitia Decidiana. He may have known her since she was a little girl, and certainly their parents had known each other; for her father, like his, was a Provençal senator. By the next summer, to their great joy, they were the parents of a son.

Agricola promptly submitted his candidature for the next step in the hierarchy: the old republican office of the quæstorship, which carried with it a seat in the Senate. By the old rules he could not have held this till his twenty-fifth year; but as a proud father he was able to take advantage of Augustus' eugenic legislation, which granted to senators a year's seniority for each of the first three legitimate children. Quæstors were elected, in former times by the people, now by the Senate; but the Emperor scrutinised the list of candidates for all offices, and sometimes only submitted as many names as there were vacancies. Nothing went wrong with this candidature, and Agricola was soon a quæstor-designate for the coming year. He was lucky, too, in the draw for the apportionment of work. A quæstor's duties were those of financial secretary to a more senior official, usually abroad; and Agricola found himself posted to "Asia" (western Asia Minor), which included the ancient and famous Greek cities east of the Ægean.

Private sorrow followed hard upon public success—the baby died. An enormous number of babies did die in the ancient world; it seems likely that, as in nineteenth-century Glasgow or Liverpool, of all the children born less than half reached the age of five. But the commonness of early death did not draw its sting, as many pathetic epitaphs bear witness.

Agricola decided to take Domitia with him to his province, a practice frowned upon by some austere critics, but perfectly legal. Ancient sea travel was neither comfortable nor safe, so, though some travellers went round Cape Matapan by "long sea", the usual route to Asia was by road to Brindisi and thence via Corinth. Fast mail went by road,

via Durazzo and Salonica; but via Corinth was the obvious
tourist route for a young couple from the north-west, deeply
interested, like most educated Romans, in the historic places
of Greece. Tacitus has no room for detailed accounts of
journeys; but it is reasonable to believe that Gnæus and
Domitia gazed and perhaps landed from their square-
rigged ship on Ithaca, the isle of Odysseus, and saw Par-
nassus and Helicon from the Corinthian Gulf, and then
presently Corinth on their right, and on their left the
shapely Perachora Mountain, and a temple beside a tiny
harbour, less famous then than now.

Ancient sea-voyagers were always glad to land, and at
Corinth, anyhow, one had to. There was no isthmus canal,
though Nero was to attempt one; sometimes ships were
hauled across a slipway on rollers, but even so they had to
be emptied; so our travellers could, if they would, visit the
archaic temple (already six hundred years old) and walk in
the modern town, and remember what they had read about
the Roman sack of ancient Corinth and the Roman consul
carrying off masterpieces of Greek art, and insisting on a
clause in his contract with the shippers, that if any were
lost in transit they should be replaced by others as
good. Above rose the towering citadel, with a splendid
view if one chose to climb it; you can see Athens on a clear
day.

There is no reason to suppose that they heard anything
about a Jew named Paulus who had lived in Corinth as a
tent-maker a few years earlier, and whose preaching had
caused a minor riot when Seneca's brother was governor.

But the chief place to see on the way to Asia was, of
course, Athens. Nearly all the ships made their first call at
Piræus; so you could, if you wished, let the heavy luggage
go on to Ephesus with most of the servants (naturally, one
travelled in a style befitting a nobleman), spend a few days
in Athens, and go on to find everything ready. So it would
be easy to visit the places famous in history and legend:
the hillside where Demosthenes and Pericles spoke; the
theatre (if it was at a festival time, one could see some
plays); the colonnade where Zeno taught the first Stoics;
the Areopagus, where the Senate of Athens debated, and

from whose top you have the best of all views of the Acropolis. The whole city was one great gallery of works of art. It must, indeed, have had an almost stunning effect, exhausting, long before one had seen everything, all powers to take in anything more. But the great, cool temple of the Parthenon reigned over all, miraculously fresh, "as though newly built", as a boy named Plutarch was just discovering. Thousands of Roman visitors, like thousands of moderns, must have climbed the steps of the Acropolis, wondering if the Parthenon could really be as good as everyone said—only to find that it was.

They stayed, of course, with friends; there was no need to bother with the indifferent hotels of antiquity. There were thousands of students in Athens, rich and poor, Greeks and Romans; and among the Romans were some of the richest young men in the empire, sons of consuls or of equestrian millionaires, living in their own houses and employing slave-secretaries to fair-copy their lecture-notes. To such, Agricola and his young wife would be welcome guests. Roman ladies were rare overseas; and Agricola himself, with the glamour of the battles in Britain upon him, would be able to satisfy the young men's curiosity for details of the campaign. With an eager circle hanging on his words, he would be able to forget any embarrassment over the fact that he had only been educated at Marseilles.

They arrived safely in Asia; and Domitia was expecting another baby.

There was plenty to see among the ancient Greek cities of Ionia too: the great Temple at Ephesus; the citadel of Pergamum, once capital of the whole region, with the huge altar, called Satan's Seat by a Christian writer not many years later. It was a war-memorial of the generation after Alexander the Great, when the Ionian Greeks, led by the Macedonian captain of Pergamum, had driven a horde of raiding Celts back into their own "Galatia" in the interior. It was adorned in florid relief with the writhing, struggling, wounded or fallen figures of Greeks and Galatians, Greeks and Persians, Greeks and Amazons, Gods and Giants—the historic and legendary struggles of civilised Europe against barbarism. Roman taste probably thought it lovely. Excavated by German archæologists, it was also much admired in Berlin. It is now in Moscow. But there was also much necessary travelling, on horseback or in one's sedan-chair on the dusty roads, in attendance on the governor, or representing him when he was wanted badly in two places; for a governor's business in a peaceful province was largely a matter of travelling on circuit, settling administrative questions with due regard to treaty- or charter-rights of local self-government, and hearing important or doubtful cases at law, civil or criminal, as supreme judge of appeal, except when a Roman citizen appealed to Cæsar. And Agricola found that, if Britain had made demands on his physical courage, his moral courage and principles could be no less severely tested here.

The great Greek and half-Greek cities of Asia were full of graft, full of venomous enmities, full of wealth and full of works of art. As a result, a governor had only to let it be seen that he was prepared to grant favours or stretch a point at law in return for bakshish, to make a fortune in a year. Things were not quite as they had been in the brave days of old, when if a governor expressed admiration of a work of art the owner was well advised to give it to him promptly; but a great deal could still be done without incurring actual prosecution on one's return to Rome. The Proconsul of Asia, L. Salvius Titianus, was a nobleman of few principles, and was having a highly profitable time. But a great many of the shady deals that could be done naturally needed, if they were to go through in strict privacy, the complicity of the financial secretary.

Agricola stuck his heels in. This was not according to his upbringing, not his idea of how a Stoic and a Roman gentleman should behave. It must have required a good deal of courage for a young man of a new and minor senatorial family to stand up to the temptations and pressure of an ex-consul and a man personally known to the Emperor. Domitia remembered it vividly; it must be from her memories of how worried he was that Tacitus, interrupting a swift and summary account of Agricola's rise through the hierarchy, inserts this episode.

The news from Rome was sensational that summer. An appalling fire burned out a great part of the centre of the city, raging among the wooden-floored tenement buildings and causing many deaths. Nero had looked on at the spectacle with too evident enjoyment; there was furious resentment among the homeless thousands, and rumour even said the emperor had burned down his own capital to make room for grandiose building projects or to inspire him for a musical composition on the sack of Troy. ("Fiddling while Rome was burning.") Nero, however, ordered effective relief measures, and dexterously shifted the blame on to the shoulders of an unpopular oriental religious sect, the Christians, who were already commonly suspected of ritual cannibalism, incest and other enormities. He arrested at least several hundreds of these, and used his considerable ingenuity in thinking up entertaining ways of killing them; a form of entertainment which, transferred to the cinematograph, has never lost its appeal —lowest depth calling to lowest depth. Christianity was thus effectively brought to the notice of a wider public than before, and Agricola, in a province where there were already seven numerous congregations, must have noticed their existence after this if not before. But the merits and demerits of an eastern sect were of less moment to him that summer than the event in his family. In the province of Asia his second child was born—a daughter; and she did not die in infancy.

As his time in Asia drew to a close, Agricola would be looking forward to taking his seat in the Senate; but acquaintances newly come from Rome hinted—it was far too dangerous a subject for a letter—that all was not well there.

Nero's government was going from bad to worse. Burrus had died in 62; Seneca had lost all influence. Nero had long since (in 59) got rid of his terrible mother by murder, and a dutiful Senate had rendered thanks to heaven for saving the Emperor from being murdered by her. He had stolen the wife of L. Salvius Otho (brother of Agricola's late chief), but, since the husband was compliant, had done nothing worse to him than send him to govern Portugal.

His immoralities were flagrant; but worse, by Roman senatorial standards, were his appearances on the stage as singer or lyre-player. Sensing himself despised, he grew touchy and suspicious of those who should have been his advisers. Remembering Gaius, he feared assassination; and soon all senators feared his suspicion and caprice.

While Agricola was on his way home, indeed, a conspiracy was hatching in good earnest; but it had too many members; some of them behaved with fantastic indiscretion; and the first major event after his return was its discovery. Then there was a reign of terror. Soldiers and spies were everywhere; there were scores of arrests; torture, executions, forced suicides. Many prominent men who were almost certainly not conspiring were forced to suicide on suspicion, or on information extracted by torture or fear, or given for rewards or through envy. One of these was Seneca; it was reported that some of the conspirators had planned to make him emperor. Another was Petronius, once Nero's arbiter of fashion, and the probable author of the *Satyricon*, a piece of brilliant fooling and the prototype of the picaresque novel.

In the circumstances it is not surprising that the Senate was a disappointment. Where any opposition to the Emperor's wishes might give offence and almost any speech might be misconstrued by an informer, the best hope of survival was in lying low. Even earlier, Claudius had complained that the Senate would not really debate. Agricola himself was in no real danger, being only a junior senator, and not a member of one of those aristocratic families who might think themselves as good as the Cæsars; indeed, since the machine of government continued to function, and since men would clearly be wanted to fill the higher commands in ten years' time, his advancement in rank continued steadily. But in the stifling atmosphere of Rome in the last years of Nero, it may well be imagined that he felt a nostalgia—not for Asia and the worrying days under Titianus, but for Britain, even with all its dark forests and grey skies: for comrades whom you knew; even for the long roads and the battlefields with a good horse under you. "He became filled," says Tacitus, "with the passion for mili-

57

tary glory"; a passion originally born, according to Tacitus, in Britain in the days of Boudicca.

In 66 Agricola was one of the ten Tribunes of the People; the ancient office had long ceased to perform any function, and now merely marked a grade in the hierarchy. One of his colleagues proposed with quixotic gallantry to veto the proceedings—the Tribune's old right—when Thrasea, a famous Stoic senator, was arraigned for treason. His chief offence was that of staying at home whenever the Senate was thanking heaven for delivering Nero from the machinations of the last person to be liquidated. Thrasea himself, however, persuaded the young man not to be foolish, and died with Stoic fortitude.

Agricola needed no persuasion. His father's fate, and his mother's advice about it, can seldom have been out of his mind in those days. If one would serve the emperor, one must bow to his ways. "To pray for a good Emperor and put up with what one got" was the beginning and end of wisdom for many a senator in the days of the Cæsars.

So the year passed, and the next year, when Agricola was merely a private senator again. In 68 he was a prætor, the rank next below that of consul. In ancient times prætors had commanded armies; more lately they had handled Rome's judicial work; and two out of the twelve elected each year still handled some. But for Agricola, by the luck of the draw, this too was merely an honorary though necessary promotion. It was also an expensive one. On reaching this rank, he had by ancient custom the sanguinary and popular duty of providing a show for the people of the capital. To produce gladiators appears by now to have been an imperial prerogative; but dancers and chariot-races would be expected, and also some large animals to be killed; preferably dangerous animals, which could be fed with condemned criminals or goaded into fighting each other, before being despatched, in the second perform-ance, by skilled so-called hunters. Such shows were no longer the straightest avenue to the great heart of the elec-torate, as in the brave days of the republic; but a good deal of prestige and popularity still depended on them. Fellow senators would help, with subscriptions in cash or kind;

Agricola's father, as we saw, had distinguished himself by not accepting *all* contributions. Even so, the task was a difficult one for a young man only moderately rich and not anxious either to run heavily into debt or to get a name for meanness; and his anxieties (and Domitia's) over striking a happy medium between extravagance and parsimony may still be divined in Tacitus' statement that he succeeded in doing so.

Nero, meanwhile, had gone to Greece in 67, where he turned, with a golden spade, the first sod of a projected Corinth canal. All the great Games were held specially, whether it was the right year for them or not, and Nero won all the prizes. He was recalled in haste by the secretary he had left in Rome; but by now nothing could have saved him. Not merely conspirators were astir, but the governors of the western provinces: first Vindex, in Gaul, a Gallic nationalist, but he was crushed by the Rhine army; then old Galba, a grandson of one of Cæsar's marshals, in Spain, supported by young Otho in Portugal. The victorious Rhine army meanwhile offered the throne to their own general, Verginius, who wisely refused it. "The secret was out," says Tacitus: "An emperor could be made elsewhere than at Rome."

Nero, not without assistance, cut his throat, aged 30, a poser to the last, with the words "What an artist dies in me!" Everyone hoped the worst was now over; actually it was just beginning.

Chapter Six

Revolution and Return to Britain

GALBA, the new emperor, gave the young prætor the first piece of public work he had had since his return from Asia—that of enquiring into thefts of artistic and other treasures from Roman temples. There had been many opportunities, provided by the great fire and the demoralised administration of the last few years. Agricola threw himself with vigour into the task, and recovered much lost property; he claimed that the only thief whose depredations he found quite irreparable was the late emperor. But before he had fairly completed this piece of work, Galba in turn was dead. He had offended his supporter Otho, by adopting another man as his destined successor, the people by unpopular austerity after Nero's extravagance, and the Guards by trying to restore discipline. On the 15th January, A.D. 69, the Guards proclaimed Otho emperor and killed Galba in the Forum.

Otho, young (about 40), able when roused, affable and easy-going, was more popular than Galba; but by now the legions on the Rhine, the largest and proudest of all the frontier armies, had already half-forced the title of emperor upon their new general, Vitellius, an elderly man, full of honours, but grown fat, slack and greedy. There were not, perhaps, many senators who had no worse faults; but his proclamation was not due to any love felt for him by his troops, but to the ambitions of subordinate officers, playing upon the men's *esprit de corps*, jealousy of the Guards and hopes of excitement and loot. Two powerful columns were soon making for the Alpine passes. Otho sent in haste for the Danube legions, which could be trusted not to give way quietly to their comrades from the Rhine; but it would be months before they could arrive in force, and in the mean time he had to make do with what troops he had. The Guards, of the strength of about two legions, were not to be despised, for all their ornamental trappings; another legion had been raised in haste from the sailors of the fleet; and the "Fighting XIVth", from Britain, was in North Italy, having been called in by Nero for a projected eastern campaign. There was no lack of generals, including Agricola's old commander, Suetonius Paulinus; "in point of fact, too many". With a brilliant staff and a scratch army, including a force of gladiators, Otho prepared to dispute the line of the Po, sending, meanwhile, his fleet to demonstrate against the flank of the Vitellians on the coast of Provence.

Agricola, so far, had managed to keep out of things. Both Otho and Vitellius were better men than Nero, but neither side provided a cause to die for. But the war was not to leave him unscathed. Otho's fleet off the Maritime Alps effected the diversion of only a few enemy auxiliary battalions for coast defence; but an enjoyable spring holiday was had by the sailors, looting the little towns and country houses on shore. At one of these an elderly lady, instead of fleeing inland, confronted the raiders; but they were not disposed to listen to argument. They killed her and looted the house. She was Agricola's mother.

By the time Agricola heard of this disaster, the fighting in Italy was over—for the moment. Otho, after a partial defeat, and while his men were still full of fight, burned his papers and committed suicide, apparently from a mixture of weariness of the life he was living and a genuine desire to save the lives of others; and the Rhine Army marched into Rome in triumph. Both piety and interest demanded that Agricola should visit his family property and make the last offerings at his mother's grave. It was no doubt a relief to escape from the conspiratorial fevers, rumours and dangers of Rome; but he had hardly completed his journey when he found himself caught up once more in stirring events. The eastern army-group, not to be out- done, had proclaimed their own emperor; their choice falling, after the governor of Syria had evaded the honour, upon Titus Flavius Vespasianus, commanding the army then engaged in suppressing a rebellion of the Jews. There had long been a persistent prophecy circulating to the effect that a ruler of the world should come from Judæa. The Jews had given it their own interpretation; but to the Romans it was now clear that they themselves had found the correct answer. The Danube legions, disappointed at the collapse of Otho, adhered to Vespasian; and daring messengers made their way through to Gaul, to spread the news and to play on western jealousies of the Rhine army.

Among the first important officials to hear this news in Gaul was the finance officer of Provence, Valerius Paulinus; a man of local influence, for he was, like Agricola, a native of Fréjus. Paulinus took up the cause of Vespasian at once. Though perhaps surprised at the elevation of one so un-aristocratic, he was at the same time delighted. Vespasian was an old friend of his, and Paulinus was convinced that he was as worthy of the position of Augustus as Vitellius, now over-eating on the Palatine, was unworthy. It was also an admirable opportunity to distinguish one's self on the winning side—if it did win. Paulinus was quick to secure the support of Agricola; an ex-prætor who was also a local magnate was an adherent worth having; and while the Danube legions poured into Italy and defeated the Rhine army, which was betrayed by its general, in furious fighting north of the Po, Valerius' men in Provence performed the important service of cutting the western route to the Rhine frontier, and capturing a Vitellian general who tried to get through by that way to bring reinforcements.

This achievement materially shortened the civil war. It also made the fortune of Agricola, who, though he does not appear to have done much personally, was able to present himself to the new emperor as an early adherent. Hitherto his career had been respectable but inconspicuous; henceforth, he was a marked man.

By the end of the year the fighting was all over; the only serious internal war in the Roman empire between 31 B.C. and A.D. 193. It had been sharp while it lasted, and destructive, but only locally. The unfortunate Vitellius was dragged out of his hiding-place in a porter's lodge and butchered by the victorious soldiers; and when Agricola reached Rome again in mid-winter he found Mucianus, the late governor of Syria who had pushed Vespasian into the place of honour, in full control. Vespasian himself, leaving his son Titus to besiege Jerusalem, had gone to secure Egypt, the chief granary of the capital, and did not reach Rome till later.

The elevation of Vespasian to the throne surprised everybody—or would have, if after a year of four Emperors anything had not seemed possible. It certainly surprised Vespasian himself. A tax-farmer's son and a centurion's grandson, he came from much the same social stratum as Agricola's father, who was a few years older than he; but though well educated he had acquired none of the social and literary polish of a Græcinus. Square-headed and bull-necked, in appearance, tastes and accent he took after his ancestors, farmers in the Sabine hills. His grandmother's farm, where he had been brought up, was his summer cottage when he was Emperor; and he flatly refused to have the place in any way altered or beautified. He had distinguished himself long ago, in command of a legion in Britain; but for the rest his official career had not been brilliant. Once at least his rural manners had got him into serious trouble; he went to sleep while Nero was singing, and was dismissed from court. Even his appointment, in the last year of Nero, to the difficult command in Palestine was probably due to the fact that his lack of polish made him "impossible" as a leader of rebellion; but now the impossible had happened. In his person, the new middle class that had emerged under the Cæsars reached the throne; and the support of men of this class, like Agricola and Valerius, who knew something of his sterling qualities, had played a great part in putting him there. His peasant shrewdness and toughness found full scope in imposing the unpopular reforms, retrenchment and heavy taxation which were necessary after the extravagances of Nero and the civil war. That done, he later found large sums for education and social services, though also, it must be added, for entertainment in the Roman manner; he built the Colosseum (of which "Coliseum" is a corruption) for gladiatorial fights, the feeding of criminals to the lions and the almost equally disgusting "huntings" of captive animals. His reign initiated, however, the most peaceful and constructive century of the Roman empire.

But before even retrenchment could begin, there were consequences of recent events to be liquidated. Titus was still besieging Jerusalem; and in the absence of half the Rhine Army, chaos had developed on that undermanned frontier. The Gallic and German native troops, formidable from their Roman training, turned against the skeleton legions, first nominally in the name of Vespasian, and then more and more openly with nationalist ideas of their own. Against them now Mucianus directed legions from Spain, from Britain (the XIVth, which had only just returned there) and from the mass of troops now in Italy. As general was chosen the dashing Cerialis, who had commanded the IXth Legion in Boudicca's rebellion, and who had also the now important qualification of being related to Vespasian. After the late heavy fighting, there was urgent need of drafts to replace casualties. Mucianus sent Agricola off on a recruiting campaign in Italy; chief recruiting officers in this metropolitan territory had to be of senatorial rank.

It was a post, like most posts in the Roman service, full of temptations. Volunteers were welcome, but insufficient in numbers. Selective conscription was necessary; and the amounts which some Roman citizens, or their parents, would pay to influence the selection were considerable. But Agricola was not to be bought. The recruits flowed out in a steady stream, and of reasonable quality. Mucianus was pleased.

After a short spell of this work, Agricola was summoned back to Rome. Mucianus was wanting a trustworthy man to take over command of XX Legion in Britain.

This was going to be difficult. The XXth had the name of being tough; in fact, at the moment they were completely out of hand. Their last general, Roscius Cœlius, had led an agitation in Vitellius' interest against the last governor appointed by Nero, who wanted to remain neutral in the civil war. This had ended in the governor being stoned off his platform, narrowly escaping murder and fleeing to the continent, while Roscius and the other two major-generals governed the province in committee. Detachments from the British legions had then fought for Vitellius in Italy. The XXth had only lately condescended to take the oath to Vespasian; the government was still in no position to apply coercion; and Roscius, now trying to restore discipline, found the task beyond him.

It was certainly going to be difficult. It must have been with mixed feelings that Agricola—though proud to be commanding a legion before his thirtieth birthday—made his way for the second time across Gaul and up the length of Watling Street.[1] Here was Britain once more : the same road and the same hills which he had passed nine years before as a smart, inexperienced young tribune fresh from the lecture-rooms at Marseilles and the advice of Seneca, long since put to death by Nero, and of his mother, brutally killed a year ago; Britain of which he had day-dreamed in the Rome of Nero, in terms of military glory; and now it was going to mean a difficult administrative position, with discipline disturbed by the cross-currents of personal and political loyalties; the sort of position in which mistakes would be easy, and in which success or failure could make or mar one's career.

London passed, and Verulam; busy water-front and inland market-place more new and raw than ever, with their wooden buildings rebuilt after the fire; and then that belt of open upland between tracts of forest, where they had so amazingly routed Boudicca's horde. One imagines Agricola stopping the convoy to have a look at the place again; and that if, as is likely, any young officers had come out from Rome with him, they would be more than willing to hear all about it. Somewhere in the south or midlands, wherever he happened to be, there would be an interview with the governor and commander-in-chief, Vettius Bolanus; a decent, uncontroversial, worried man,

---

[1] Exactly where the XXth lay at this time is uncertain; but since Leg. II, throughout its career in Britain, was based in the south-west, and Leg. IX in the east, it is clear that the only other legion in Britain must have been in the central sector. Wroxeter, at least since the departure of the XIVth, is a possibility. The fortress of Chester, it is now known, was later.

appointed by Vitellius and left in charge so far by Vespasian's government, but acutely conscious of having got a difficult situation imperfectly in hand.

Then at last, as his journey's end, there were the entrenched lines and hutted streets of the cantonment; headquarters, with the senior centurions saluting smartly and turning critical eyes upon the new general.

Agricola had made up his mind to have no nonsense, but also not to quarrel unnecessarily. He understood perfectly well what the men, who had fought, or whose comrades had fought, for Vitellius, must be feeling. On the other hand, the new government was firmly in the saddle by now, and so long as there was no vindictive penalisation, no sensible soldier was likely to make trouble for it. Agricola made no reference to the stoning of Bolanus' predecessor, nor to any other painful recent events. It must have been a great help that he *could* talk, on occasions when it was suitable to unbend, about Anglesey and Boudicca and the old days under Suetonius. In due course he reported, doubtless to the great relief of his centurions, not that he had restored discipline, but simply that XX Legion was in good shape.

All the same, he could not help feeling privately that what the troops really needed to restore morale was a good frontier war.

That, unfortunately, was impossible for the present. The frontier was still where Suetonius had found it; the army had been reduced to three legions, plus attached troops; and also the old policy of maintaining good relations with the Brigantes had finally broken down.

Thereby hangs the third and last chapter of the saga of Queen Cartimandua. Long ago, in the forties, she and her consort Venutius had made friendship with Rome their policy, had received Roman aid, probably against their own tribesmen of the anti-Roman party, and had handed over Caratacus. In the fifties, the Queen's adultery with Vellocatus had sent the injured husband, with his formidable military prowess and prestige, over to the nationalists; and with her position thus weakened, it had required a serious Roman effort, including the despatch of a legion, to re-establish her in power. With their help Venutius was driven north; but the events of the year 69 gave him his opportunity. With a force raised among the northern tribes, he crossed the Cheviots; the Brigantes rallied to him; Cartimandua found herself with little support and appealed again to the Romans. Bolanus sent a cavalry and light infantry force; with only three legions, less the detachments sent to Vitellius, he dared not adventure one of them north of the Humber. The result was some chequered fighting, of which the best is made in an elegant poem by the courtly poet Statius, addressed to Bolanus' son; but the net result of it was that the Romans rescued their ally, the now ageing queen, and took her south with them on their withdrawal. She now vanishes from history. Venutius was left in power in Northumbria. He did not invade the south; but henceforth the Roman province had a definitely hostile northern frontier.

So Agricola, pacing the courtyard of his headquarters on the north-west marches had to curb his enthusiasm and set himself to training the legion, including its large new drafts, with route-marches and battle-drills and reconnaissances along the edge of the hill country. Roman territory extended as far as Flintshire, and mining was beginning there, supervised by junior procurators of the financial service. An extant pig of lead bears a date equivalent to A.D. 74. This service was quite separate from the main military-and-political branch, reporting, as we have seen, through its own channels direct to the Emperor; but the military could be called upon to provide guards for mines and convoys, and with the mountain tribes still free and hostile, this would be no small matter.

The G.O.C. XXth Legion would also probably—since the Roman navy was an extremely junior service—exercise supervision over the Irish Sea flotilla, which it is reasonable to believe had been kept in being on the Dee since the days of Suetonius.

By reconnaissance or, less probably, from the reports of traders, Rome already knew, before the conquests of Agricola, a great deal about the Irish Sea and the western islands. Pliny the Elder, the encyclopædist, who died when Agricola was beginning his advance into Scotland, was able years before his death to put on record data about the relative sizes of Albion (Great Britain) and Ireland, the name of the Caledonian Forest and the names of many of the lesser isles. Monapia (the Isle of Man), Dumna (the Long Island) and "the thirty Æbudes", of which the name "Hebrides" is a mediæval mis-spelling, are among the names now first added to the map. The collation of topographical intelligence could be then as now a congenial occupation for an ambitious officer on a temporarily quiet frontier.

For the rest, a legion-commander on a remote frontier was necessarily a lonely man. He must have felt particularly dependent, during that year, on the mails from home, especially the letters from Domitia and the little Julia, now seven years old.

News from the rest of the empire was reasonably good. Cerialis had practically finished on the Rhine—though rumour had it that he had run an entirely characteristic risk on one occasion, when the Germans in a surprise attack nearly caught him in his night attire; and furthermore, not inside his lines, but in pursuit of his private affairs in a neighbouring town. Tacitus, who retails this information, does not seem to have liked Cerialis, though he respected his energy; but he does report a speech of his to the surrendered Gauls, on the choice between the Roman peace, with Rome's taxation and promotion for merit, and the alternative of inter-tribal anarchy, which stands as the best extant apologia for Roman imperialism. Farther afield, Titus had taken Jerusalem and settled the Jewish problem; it had to be settled with equal violence twice more in the next seventy years. At Rome, Vespasian had presented a grim post-war financial statement to a resigned but gloomy Senate. It would require 40,000,000,000 sesterces to make the State solvent (four sesterces were the maximum wage for a daily labourer). Intelligent Romans felt that they now knew the worst. Unintelligent Romans, of course, blamed the government. Vespasian who, with all his great qualities, lacked glamour, was never really popular.

Then came the great news: Cerialis, fresh from his victory on the Rhine, was to be the next governor of Britain. This could only mean one thing: the resumption of a forward policy. From the positions which they had held since the days of Ostorius, the legions were to advance again to complete the conquest of the island. The irksome period of waiting was at an end.

Chapter Seven

New Conquests in Britain

VESPASIAN, who looked at all problems with the eye of a tax-collector and who knew better than any man the need for economy, certainly did not adopt a forward policy in Britain merely for the sake of *gloire militaire*. He must have calculated that it would, in a phrase popular with modern generals, "pay a dividend". To hold and defend the Lowland Zone, as the empire was now doing, an army of three legions plus auxiliaries was barely sufficient; but if increased by one-third, the army could take the offensive; and then, once the whole island was pacified, a great reduction of the garrison might be possible. In Spain, a land almost equally isolated, this policy had already borne fruit. The three legions left there after the completion of the conquest by Augustus were reduced under Vespasian to one, stationed at Leon (which is the word "Legion") in the mountainous north-west; municipal self-government on the Roman model was being rapidly extended, and the peninsula remained happy in having no military history until the beginning of the barbarian invasions. To this hope of economy in the long run could be added the prospect of increased exploitation of the mineral wealth of the British Highland Zone. Gold and silver were still hoped for; and if the yield of these proved disappointing, there was a large output of lead. This is the branch of Romano-British mining of which we know most, by reason of the considerable number of pigs of lead, stamped often with the date and the name of their place of origin, which were lost in transit in boggy country and have been recovered in modern times.

The new reinforcements were sent over in time for the campaign of 71. They included a whole legion; not XIV this time, but one of two new formations raised from the Mediterranean fleets during the civil war. It was named the Second, Adiutrix ("assistant" or "auxiliary"; cf. our word "adjutant"). Romans when raising new units or formations usually tended to begin again at one, which resulted in much duplication of low numbers in their army list. There were thus now two Second Legions in Britain, the new Adiutrix and the old "Augustus' Own", whose headquarters had remained in the south-west ever since the days when Vespasian commanded it.

Cerialis himself arrived probably in the spring, and Agricola, doubtless at a conference of legion-commanders, heard what was in his mind. It might have been expected that the plan would be first to take in Wales, and then to push northwards; but that was not Cerialis' intention. He intended to go straight for the Brigantes, the most power-ful tribe in the whole island. The serious blow dealt to Roman prestige by Venutius in 69 may have had some-thing to do with this decision, at a governmental level; but there was also another point which must have weighed with Cerialis personally. He, most impetuous of men, had commanded the IXth at Lincoln in his younger days; he had gazed across the lower Trent into their country and seen their hills on a clear day; he had discussed routes and resources with centurions and veterans who had been over those hills during Nasica's operations in support of Carti-mandua; he had strained at the leash when Suetonius, his commander-in-chief, went off into Wales and left him to mind the back areas; and then Boudicca's rebellion had put an end, it might easily have been for ever, to all thoughts of a campaign in Northumbria.

Cerialis went, in short, straight back to his old legion, and straight ahead with what Suetonius and Boudicca had not allowed him to do. With his old Legion IX and the newcomers, II Adiutrix, he would advance, probably across the Humber at Brough and along the edge of the Yorkshire Wolds, where the Roman road still runs. He would thus cut off and perhaps "liberate", willy-nilly, the chariot-driving Parisi of the East Riding; and he would establish a new advanced base on the Ouse, which would be convenient for water-transport, not far short of the Brigantian lowland centre of Isurium (on the Ure, and probably named after the river). This would deprive the Brigantes in the Pennines (their very name appears to mean "men of the braes") of their chief granary, the Vale of the Ouse and the eastern lowlands; and if the Brigantes wanted to dispute possession of it, they would have to come down and fight a pitched battle on the plain, which was what the Romans wanted, too. The new base would be held through the winter by the seasoned Legion IX; and meanwhile the rawer troops of II, Adiutrix, who had only been one winter away from the Mediterranean, could have the old cantonments at Lincoln. (We infer this from the fact that they have left their traces there, in the shape of two or three surviving tombstones of legionaries, who died probably at the base during the winter.)

During these operations II, Augusta, would be responsible for the Welsh Marches. Legion XX—here one imagines Agricola pricking up his ears—would have an essential part to play in the campaign. This would be to advance by the western route north of the Dee, and secure the western ends of the chief routes through the Pennines. This would deny to the hill-men food-supplies from the western lowlands, and prepare to stop the bolt-holes during the second phase of the campaign—a pincer movement upon the enemy strongholds in the hill-country.

So that was it. Agricola was not overjoyed; he and his legion were not to be part of the main striking force, as he might have expected, and as they would have been if the programme had started with a resumption of Suetonius' advance into Wales. For the first year at least, they were merely to be the anvil to Cerialis' hammer— probably a stationary anvil, once the prearranged positions were taken up; for to synchronise the operations of two moving forces coming from opposite directions would have been practically impossible. However, it was an independent command, of a sort; and later, when he and Cerialis knew each other better, he realised that the commander-in-chief had been justified in not assigning too ambitious a rôle to a young general, whose capacity in major operations remained to be proved. In that summer he was, in fact, on trial.

As to details of the operations, Tacitus tells us nothing in the biography, and his *Histories* are unfortunately lost after the autumn of the year 70. We have from him only the bare facts that Cerialis attacked the Brigantes and that Agricola was in command of a column. Inscriptions show us that Legion IX, formerly at Lincoln, formed the earliest known garrison of York, while II, Adiutrix, makes a brief appearance, probably now, with winter quarters at Lincoln. Agricola's Legion XX must therefore, as always when we hear of it, have been responsible for the north-western sector. Pincer movements through the Pennines are indicated by the geography of the country and the fact that two columns were operating; and the cutting off of successive belts of conquered country by forts, served by lateral roads through the dales, is indicated by the existence of the roads and forts, though not every Roman fort in the Pennines is of this date. Mamucium (Manchester), of which Mancunium is an ancient mis-spelling, probably was; the name would be derived from the *mamelon* or breast-shaped hill on which the fort stood. From it a road later ran north-east over the moors past the high forts at Castleshaw and Slack, almost as straight for York as if on a compass-bearing.

Two marches farther north, the fort of Bremetennacum ("Loudwater") at Ribchester, in the jaws of Ribblesdale, dates from about this time, and would perform a similar function. It commanded the western approach to the Aire Gap, the lowest pass from Lancashire into Yorkshire. From it another moorland road ran due east, with forts at Elslack and Ilkley, the ancient Olicana. Converging on York, the two roads met at Calcaria, "The Limestone Quarries", now Tadcaster. Between Manchester and Ribchester the "Red Fort" of Coccium (Wigan?) maintained communications. Finally, and later, after Agricola's time, a "Pennine Way" of obvious strategic usefulness ran south from Ilkley, over the "wuthering heights" above Keighley and Haworth, to Blackstone Edge and Manchester.

By holding Manchester in force with patrols out to the

AGRICOLA

Pennine crest, the XXth would be fulfilling their strategic rôle, preparing the way for an "annihilation battle", when the main army from York marched westward. A major objective must have been the great Brigantian stronghold of Camulodunum, "Fort of Camulos" the war-god, at Almondbury, near Huddersfield.

At the end of the campaign, Agricola seems to have been disappointed at the amount of notice he got in Cerialis' despatches. He had had, he felt, a full share in the danger and responsibilities of the year, and was not getting much of the credit. However, he carried on without complaining—he was certainly a much better subordinate than many Roman senators—and he had his reward. Having found him efficient, Cerialis continued him in command of the western column in the second year, with larger forces, i.e. with more cavalry and light infantry attached to his legion, and with a proportionately more important rôle; and also gave handsome recognition to his services when reporting to Rome. Agricola was thus able to pose with becoming modesty as "only a subordinate" without, says Tacitus, losing the credit for his actions.

The years 72 and 73 saw the Roman columns penetrate to the far north of the Brigantian country, perhaps even into Scotland; but only at the cost of savage and sometimes costly fighting. A vast Brigantian entrenchment at Stanwick in North Yorkshire was stormed; but any hopes of a *Vernichtungsschlacht* were disappointed. The light-armed, swift-moving hillmen made good their escape. The sufferings of the tribe, whose only offence was an objection to foreign rule, must have been terrible; but year after year they still rallied again.

As the advance continued, its difficulties increased; the country grew ever wilder, the hills rising to miniature mountains on left and right. Agricola with the western column will have had his first sight of the fells of Cumberland. Communications lengthened; serious problems arose over consolidation. The usual procedure was to plant forts at the nodal points of communication, at the fork of a major valley or the summit of a pass, and to leave an auxiliary cohort with some tough centurions to spend the winter in each and keep an eye on the district; but to hold such a post through a winter among the Brigantes was no light matter. At some places, when the legions advanced again in the late, wet spring of the north country they found no post to relieve—only the charred ruins of hut-ments, ditches and ramparts fiercely levelled, and scattered bones gnawed by wolves. Sometimes, too, a dishevelled and humiliated remnant of a garrison would straggle in at "Legion", as the Romans called a legionary base, desper-ately prepared to face the worst the general might do to them, having been starved or intimidated into agreeing to surrender their outpost and save their lives. The enemy became accustomed in fact, says Tacitus, to win back in the winter what they lost in the summer. It is partly a Tacitean gibe, contrasting Cerialis with the author's hero; but it must be based on some facts. Rome's wars in Britain begin at this point, as they enter the highland zone, to be in-creasingly reminiscent of the campaigns of mediæval English kings: the sweeps of heavily armed English armies into Scotland alternating with long-drawn Scottish re-covery of the castles by surprise or grim siege or perilous escalade.

How far Cerialis finally penetrated is uncertain; his ad-vanced columns may even have entered Scotland, but he certainly did not consolidate so far as that. There were even some loose ends about his conquest of the Brigantes, if we may judge by another saying of Tacitus—that "the greater part of the tribal territory was conquered, or at least invaded". However, his was certainly a considerable achievement, and one which, to quote Tacitus again, "struck terror" into all anti-Roman hearts. Hitherto men might have felt that the Romans shirked a frontal attack on that powerful tribe, but never again now.

After three years, or four years including his summer on the Rhine, Cerialis was recalled. An inscription of May, 74, shows that the Emperor conferred on him the exceptional honour of a second consulship, and only four years after his first. The tremendous hammer-and-tongs of the fight-ing in Yorkshire had raised his reputation to a great height—high enough, indeed, to make him a difficult man to succeed. But Vespasian, with considerable imagination, had a successor ready, both adequate and in the strongest possible contrast to the dashing Cerialis.

Sextus Julius Frontinus, the tenth governor of Britain, was an intellectual soldier, a skilled engineer and surveyor, an authority, in later years, on the aqueducts of the city of Rome, on which he wrote a book which can still be read. He also wrote a two-volume manual of *Military Science* (Vol. I: *Organisation*; Vol. II: *Tactics*), but it is unfortunately lost, and we have to be content, as a specimen of his military writing, with a collection of *Stratagems*, a form of light literature for practical men which seems to have been popular. It is simply a collection of stories from history illustrating useful dodges, and not omitting psychological warfare—due attention to the morale of one's own men, and attacks on that of the enemy. Nor does Frontinus fail to deal with the subject of military secrecy, as in a pleasant anecdote of Metellus Pius, a famous general of the Republic, in Spain. One of his young officers asked him which way he was going to march next morning, and received the terse answer: "If my shirt knew, I'd burn it."

Frontinus' work in Britain was complementary to that of Cerialis, not a continuation of it. With his engineer's preference for giving first priority to foundations, he declined to invade Scotland before making an end in Wales. He concentrated three legions for this task, bringing over II, Adiutrix, to a new post on the western marches at Chester. Fifteen of its tombstones, compared with three at Lincoln, show that II, Adiutrix, was based at Chester during the greater part of its sojourn in Britain.

With these and thousands of auxiliaries—25,000 to 30,000 men in all—in three years of grim, methodical warfare, Frontinus bore down the brave Silures. Their great stronghold overlooking the Bristol Channel from the hills above Caerwent, with its fortifications significantly strengthened at the time of the first Roman invasion, now fell at last and was dismantled. Legion II, Augusta, was brought forward to winter at Isca (named from the River Usk), denying to the hill-men the use of winter pastures in the coastal plain. A string of coastal forts, which could be supplied by sea from the estuaries, continued the process farther west: Nidum, Leucarum, Maridunum, whose names survive in Neath, Loughor, and Carmarthen. One is reminded of the similar part played by the Welsh castles of Anglo-Norman kings. Finally the Roman roads, with battalion-forts at every day's march, were driven relentlessly through the heart of the Silurian hills: up the Usk from Gobannium (Abergavenny), where stamped tiles show a detachment of the legion established, to Y Gaer—"The Fort"—of Brecon, in its valley-head, where a "wing" of cavalry, from northern Spain, was installed; and so right on to the coast of Cardigan Bay, past the gold-mine at Dolaucothy. From Brecon again roads ran north into Mid-Wales, north-east to the Wye, south-west to Neath and south-east to Cardiff via the fort at Gellygaer. At this last a pair of inscriptions shows building work both by the legion and, probably, by a Pannonian battalion,[1] no doubt the permanent occupants.

The work was done later, in peace-time; but the co-operation of skilled legionary craftsmen with the auxiliaries, themselves growing continually more "regular" and disciplined, in establishing strong and permanent stone forts, is typical of a reform initiated by Frontinus. He too, it appears, had taken to heart the reverses sustained in winter warfare by Roman outposts in the days of Cerialis; and the powerfully fortified, virtually impregnable cohort-posts, which were to be a feature of Agricola's methods of consolidation, first appear in Wales and in his time.

Broken at last, the Silures sued for peace, and with politic magnanimity were permitted to retain their identity as a tribe. Their hill-fort in Llanmelin Woods is replaced by Caerwent, Venta of the Silures, down in the plain, with the legion at Caerleon lying between it and

[1] Definitely not Spaniards—a possibility which used to give restorers pause. The stone is broken, but comparison with the companion inscription (for the two are a pair) shows that there could not have been room for the Emperor's titles and the word "Cohort", even abbreviated, and the syllables HISPAN—.

the tribal hinterland. At a county-council level, the "Republic of the Silures" was still active in the third century, and Caerwent was one of the most durable of British towns, preserving indeed a shadow of urban life far into the dark ages. But like the tribal capital of the Iceni— another Venta—it was a very small capital.

Chapter Eight

Governor of Aquitaine

AGRICOLA did not serve under Frontinus. He was recalled, perhaps at the same time as Cerialis; and there
was an honour for him too. Vespasian and Titus were
holding, in 73–74, the ancient magistracy of the Censor-
ship, one of whose functions was to recruit the Senate
when depleted, and to purge it of unworthy members; and
they were also filling up the depleted ranks of the oldest
nobility of Rome—the Patricians. Patrician and plebeian
had ceased to be the really operative class-distinction of
Rome nearly four centuries ago; but even now patricians
alone were qualified to hold certain ancient priesthoods
and perform their antique rites, on which Augustus, with
the emphasis on history characteristic of a patriotic revolutionary, had laid great stress. A patrician, then, Agricola now became. The idea of a patrician of partly Gaulish
descent may well have caused some of the Fathers of
primitive Rome to turn in their graves. It was, however,
no doubt a tribute to Agricola's social presentability and
refinement (greatly exceeding Vespasian's own, as Vespasian
was amusedly aware) that Agricola was among those
selected for this particular form of ennoblement.

Along with this rather pleasing and recherché honour
came also a good mundane promotion. The Emperor desired him, with effect from some date probably in 74, to
take over the governorship of Aquitaine.

This was excellent. Immediate or almost immediate re-
employment was good in itself; and while there were
some eight provinces to which an ex-prætor might be
posted, between his command of a legion and reaching
the consulship, Aquitaine was generally if informally
recognised as one of the best. It was a post which was

often followed by an early consulship. Aquitaine at 34 was the best possible sign that the Emperor thought well of him.

Also, Aquitaine was a province where one could take one's wife, and Agricola and Domitia, having probably had no home life during his three years with a legion, no doubt appreciated that. It could not indeed be proved that Agricola did *not* take Domitia with him to Britain; but the Welsh marches in A.D. 71 do not sound a very suitable place for a lady. They could take the little Julia to Aquitaine too. She was ten years old now; by the time they saw Rome again it would be time to see about getting her married.

The governorship of Aquitaine was a new experience for Agricola in several ways.

First of all there was the country and its people. Considering that it was only across the Cevennes from Provence, it was surprisingly different. It was Atlantic or inland, rather than Mediterranean; and it was far less completely Romanised. In most of Provence the units of local government were the new towns, the Roman colonies. In the west the Gallic tribes or cantons were preserved and utilised. Nîmes, Narbonne, Avignon are names of ancient towns, Nemausus, Narbo, Avennio, though Nîmes was a tribal capital too; but Tarbes, Poitiers, Limoges preserve the names of pre-Roman tribes. Provence supplied the army with citizen legionaries; Aquitaine supplied auxiliary units, one of which, a First Aquitaine Cohort, was policing Derbyshire in the second century, and was probably already in Britain in Agricola's time.

There was no army in Aquitaine itself, nor any likelihood of trouble. Like all Gaul, except the Old Province, and like all the other less civilised or frontier districts of the empire, it was one of "Cæsar's provinces"; part of the vast "province" or sphere of action which his faithful senators had made over to Augustus at the end of the revolutionary period. The governor's title therefore was not Proconsul but Legate—in full, "Legate of Augustus" The Proconsul was the Emperor himself.

But Roman ways of life spread rapidly; it was soon possible to leave local police work to the native authorities, with the Rhine army in the background; though there may possibly have been a handful of legionaries seconded from the Rhine in attendance on the governor.

New, too, was the feeling of being in charge, with no one over one except the emperor; though it had something in common with being in charge of a legion for the first time, especially when it was the tough XXth directly after the civil war. There was the feeling of being on probation again too. If he could do well at the administrative and judicial work of a governor, having already given satisfaction in his command of a legion, then he really would be marked for higher command.

It *might* even mean the command in Britain.

On the other hand, reports would soon reach Rome if he failed. Naturally, plenty of people were envious of his quick promotion; and even friends would agree that hitherto he had only proved himself as a soldier. "Most people," says Tacitus at this point, "consider that the military mind is lacking in subtlety." It is indeed exactly the sort of judgment that Tacitus himself, elsewhere, might delicately hint. However, he assures us that Agricola's natural good sense enabled him to combine justice and adaptability in dealing with civilians.

The work of a governor in a peaceful province like Aquitaine was largely judicial. All criminal cases involving a capital sentence came before him, for the native courts were not allowed to put any man to death; and there were also numerous civil cases, either particularly important or particularly difficult or liable to create a precedent, as when native custom had to be harmonised with Roman ideas on equity. The governor was the ultimate court of appeal on all questions, except those involving the life or status of a Roman citizen, who might appeal to Cæsar. For reference, he had the body of case-law represented by the decisions of his predecessors; probably also the larger body of case-law summarised (but not codified) in the annual Edict of the City Prætor at Rome; and he had a staff of experienced slave clerks who would know where to find things in the already well-stocked files. With that

81

and his natural common sense, fortified by such legal knowledge as would come the way of every senator—a member of a class and people who enjoyed their law— Agricola, like other Roman governors, had to "make do". If in serious doubt he could refer to Rome, and the Emperor, after consultation with such legal luminaries as he chose, would send him the answer. These answers are the *rescripts*, which figure prominently in the later Roman law-books. But one would not want to do this all the time; the amount of work which Vespasian already undertook personally would have killed most men, and he preferred his Legates to take responsibility. Nor were the cases presented in a manner calculated to save the governor's time. Educated Gauls took very kindly to all that was worst in Latin prose composition: its rhetorical tricks, its straining after effect, its tendency to prize point and antithesis above clarity. The advocates were undeniably clever; they fastened swiftly upon any point of law likely to help their case. Agricola must often have thought longingly of what Tacitus calls the rough-and-ready military justice of his tribunal at legionary headquarters.

However, business in Aquitaine rarely had the immediate urgency to which Agricola had grown used in the army; and it was possible here at least to keep regular hours. After playing the part, on the judgment-seat, of the stern and keen-witted judge, letting nothing pass, but often tempering justice with mercy, he could adjourn the court for the day, unbend and be himself without further standing on official dignity.

Apart from legal business, conducted on tour at the chief tribal centres and wherever else the governor might happen to be, there was much formal and informal work of a kind familiar to the eminent in all ages: inspecting new public buildings, roads and bridges, for example—not actually laying foundation-stones or declaring places open, but it came to the same thing; replying, in a few well-chosen words, to addresses of welcome from Gallic chieftains, transformed by Roman law into Roman landlords and county councillors; or gracefully accepting the hospitality of local magnates, delighted, though a little alarmed, at having the honour to entertain the governor. Above all, it was a governor's business to encourage all tendencies that made for Romanisation; especially the official cult of "Rome and the Emperor", which had sprung up in the east spontaneously in the days of Augustus, the restorer of peace after the great civil wars, and had been officially encouraged as the only spiritual bond of union in the far-flung and polyglot empire. It was important, in this connection, always to be in some important centre, such as Bordeaux, on the emperor's birthday and accession day. The younger Pliny's letters to his emperor from Asia Minor include a number of formal, carefully drafted, loyal messages for these occasions, the "loyal telegrams" of those days, felicitating the emperor and assuring him of the dutiful prayers of his people for his continued preservation in health and strength for the well-being of the world.

Much time was thus spent on tour, especially during the warm and comparatively rainless summer. Aquitaine was a huge province; as delimited by Augustus, it included not only Aquitaine proper but all Gaul up to the Loire, including Bourges, the capital of the Bituriges, and the Hot Springs (Vichy). This vast tract of the Centre had been added in order to make the province roughly the same size as the next—Lugdunensis or Lyonnais, a great belt of territory extending from Lyons, the centre of all Gaul, to Brittany. Aquitaine thus included a great variety of peoples and ways of life: the shepherds of Auvergne, the rich farmers of the plains, the merchants and sailors of Bordeaux, and in the far south-west, outside the Gallic area, the Aquitani proper—dark Iberians, quite different from the red- or brown-haired Gauls, and speaking a very different language, full of aspirates and Ls and Rs and Xs in improbable combinations.

There was a certain amount of irritation among these Iberians at being thrown in with a large Gallic population who were not Aquitani at all. It was felt that their voice could not be heard properly in the provincial council, which, though denied any power over the administration, did possess the important right to make representations, on matters of common interest, to the governor or even to

Rome. Not many years later, they sent a deputation to Rome and obtained the right to a separate council within the province. Consciousness of not being Celts did not, however, diminish the pride felt by their leading men in being Roman citizens. When the deputation got back, its leader commemorated his achievement on the mausoleum which he was building for himself, in four lines of indifferent verse—but in Latin. It is significant, though Tacitus does not comment on it, that Agricola, who was to do so much for the Romanisation of Britain, had this recent experience of what peace under Roman government could make of a mainly Celtic land.

What Tacitus does comment on as a feature of his hero's first governorship is that he studiously avoided inter-departmental quarrels. Such quarrels notoriously can occur in any public service; but it does seem that they must have been unduly common in the Roman empire. Some officers of the senatorial class, men of lineage no less lofty than that of the Cæsars, suffered acute feelings of frustration from the consciousness that there was one over them whom they must never cease to treat as a superior, on pain of death. Such feelings make men all the more touchy about petty matters of precedence, and rivalries between the governors of the "Three Gauls", Aquitaine, Lugdunensis and Belgica, which all met at Lugdunum, seem to have been common. Even more undignified were departmental battles with the financial service. Being a junior grade, both officially and socially, the equestrian finance officials were naturally even more sensitive about their rights and those of their service; and the functions and duties of the financial service overlapped those of the political and administrative service at many points. The crafty Augustus had been at no pains to remove such causes of friction. It suited him well that they should exist, and that his trusty bourgeois tax-collectors and estate-managers should be willing as well as able to report to him privately on the doings of noble and perhaps ambitious generals and governors.

With his usual sound sense and easy temper, the young Agricola kept clear of such pitfalls. He did not demand credit for everything, even though fame is frequently, as Tacitus anticipating Milton puts it, a weakness even of the good: and as for departmental feuds, he considered, says Tacitus, that in them there was no glory in victory and only squalor in defeat. Vespasian, one of whose leading characteristics was impatience of nonsense, was duly pleased. Agricola had not been in Aquitaine for even three full years, the usual minimum in one of Cæsar's provinces, when he received notice that his successor was being appointed. Evidence that this was a sign of satisfaction was supplied by a simultaneous intimation that if he presented himself at Rome as a candidate for the consulship, his candidature would be favourably regarded. Prospects of the consulship, which gave entry to the highest rank in the hierarchy, would have to be hinted at in some such circumlocutory fashion, because the consulship, unlike the great commands to which it might lead, was nominally not in the gift of the emperor, but of the Senate; though in practice everyone knew that the emperor approved or disapproved candidatures, and that his will, if he chose to express it, was decisive.

Agricola and his family got back to Rome some time in 77 to find gossip actively canvassing the prospect that he would be the next governor of Britain. Tacitus even suggests that public opinion may have prompted his selection, which, under an emperor like Vespasian, is most unlikely. In the mean time, it was very embarrassing, but there was nothing to do about it except to keep one's mouth shut and look modest. Agricola formally announced his candidature for the consulship, and the Emperor—the "Generalissimo", preserving the polite fiction that he was merely the first citizen of the republic—permitted it to be known that he was in favour of this candidate.

Vespasian had aged noticeably in the seven years since he had entered Rome as Cæsar. He was now sixty-seven, and quite bald; Titus, a plump and polished edition of his father, whose lack of refinement he regretted, was associated with him in all his official positions. Titus was about Agricola's age. But the old man had lost none of his caustic wit, and still got through an astonishing amount of work, getting up at all hours—sometimes at midnight, after going to bed at dusk—in order to have a few undisturbed hours at his desk before a Roman gentleman's usual official levée, with a host of callers, at dawn. One of his chief cronies, and a permitted visitor during the small hours, was the elder Pliny, who by the help of a staff of shorthand clerks managed to combine the occupations of a senior administrative official with the compilation of an encyclopædia. Vespasian might lack glamour, but he was a man to work for.

While the interval between announcement of candidature and formal election pursued its decorous way, Agricola and Domitia had time to consider the important question of a husband for Julia, who had reached the mature age of thirteen. She had, no doubt, a host of suitors; for the daughter of a general high in the imperial favour and about to become consul at thirty-seven was as brilliant a match as could be found short of the imperial family. Also, since Agricola after fifteen years of married life had no other child living, she was likely to be an heiress; and Roman society was intensely, indeed morbidly, legacy-conscious. They could probably have betrothed her without difficulty to a scion of one of the surviving ancient noble houses; but preferring brains and personal promise to other qualifications, they selected instead a brilliant young man interested in history and oratory: P. Cornelius Tacitus, probably son or nephew of a man of that name mentioned in Pliny's encyclopædia as lately finance officer of Belgica; one of the many sons of equestrian families whom Vespasian and Titus had lately accepted for the senatorial class and service. As Consul—a title still full of prestige inherited from the historic past—Agricola celebrated the formal betrothal. To be marrying the daughter of a consul, and moreover a very brilliant consul, who had campaigned with Cerialis in Britain, must have been for the historically-minded Tacitus the culmination of his life to date; nor would anyone have been more pleased than the proud parents if they had known that by their choice of a son-in-law they were assuring for their name and fame a monument more enduring than bronze.

Agricola's consulship lasted probably for three or four months, early in 78, though not at the very beginning of the year. Three or four months were a normal duration of the consulship at this time, so that more men might hold the office in order to qualify for the high commands. He had left Britain with Cerialis early in 74, and had spent less than three years in Aquitaine, so that he may, if he spent very little time in Rome between appointments, have been consul in 77; but it seems likely, for reasons which will appear later (p. 134), that the seven summers of his command in Britain were those of 78 to 84 inclusive, and not earlier; and he arrived in Britain after mid-summer and soon after his consulship.

In 78, then, we will hereafter assume, Agricola held his brief consulship, and took the chair at meetings of the Senate unless Vespasian or Titus were present. That over, he celebrated, in style befitting his consular rank, the marriage of Julia to Tacitus. Then came the day of his formal appointment to the command in Britain—no doubt informally adumbrated by the Emperor some time before. With it came another mark of favour: appointment to a vacant place in the ancient priestly College of the Pontifices, of which the Emperor was always head; a position customarily filled by leading soldiers and statesmen, including such un-sacerdotal figures as Julius Cæsar.

So Agricola came within sight of his highest ambition, which was to be the man who completed the conquest of Britain. Vespasian also was heartily in favour of the forward policy; so much so that, appreciating that Britain was becoming a very large province, and that arrears of legal work would accumulate while Agricola was on campaign in the north, he seems to have invented a new senior post on the governor's staff: the post of law-officer of Britain, first heard of about this time. There was a courageous barrister of knightly status, one L. Salvius Liberalis, who had dared to defend a very rich Greek in serious trouble with the government, with all the sleuth-hounds of the empty treasury baying for his blood. Prosecuting counsel even seems to have hinted that his confiscated estate would be a nice windfall; whereat Salvius cried out: "Is it any concern of Cæsar's if Hipparchus *is* a millionaire?" Everyone expected Salvius to be arraigned for *lèse-majesté*; but Vesparian, on the contrary, promoted him to the Senate with prætorian rank, and sent him as law officer to Britain about the beginning of the governorship of Agricola.[1]

About midsummer 78, with high hopes and ambitious plans, Agricola took leave of Vespasian, and for the third time set out for Britain.

[1] E. B. Birley believes that Salvius went to Britain rather later, in 81. If so, he was sent out by Titus, probably in answer to a request from Agricola himself.

Chapter Nine

Governor of Britain

IT was late summer when Agricola reached Britain, and the troops had made up their minds that there would be no major operations that year; the new governor would want to take his time going round the province, seeing how things were and making speeches. When Agricola arrived, however, he found a situation requiring prompt action. Frontinus, with his roads and forts, had dealt finally with the Silures; one is reminded once more of Edward I and his Welsh castles. But as in the Middle Ages, the natural fortress of Snowdonia was the last to fall. The Ordovices had risen in arms, and the first news that greeted the new governor was of a regrettable incident. They had caught a Roman cavalry "wing" on unfavourable ground, presumably in one of their mountain passes, and virtually destroyed it. The news, spreading rapidly, had sent a thrill through the newly conquered tribes. If the defeat was not quickly avenged, there was danger that instead of completing the conquest of Britain, the new governor would find himself beating out the embers of guerilla warfare in districts already overrun by Frontinus and Cerialis.

The army was in its winter positions, spread out as an occupying force through most of Wales and Northumbria; to mobilise it in full strength would take weeks, and there would not be much left of the summer. But Agricola, knowing the country, knew also that the numerical strength of the Ordovices was not very great. The chief problem was presented by the roughness of their country. Speed and decisive action were imperative; large numbers of armoured men were not. He wrote, probably from London, to his legion-commanders for detachments, which could be sent off much more easily than the main body of the legions, to concentrate at some suitable point, such as Chester. With these detachments (probably 2,000 men from each legion) and with such cavalry and light infantry as could be most easily concentrated, he pushed rapidly westwards, and within a few weeks of landing he brought the hillmen to bay. Personally leading his troops on foot, he directed the assault which burst through their defences— evidently those of a hill-fort. There was fearful carnage; to the Roman public as much a matter for satisfaction as Omdurman to the Victorians. The Ordovices were eliminated as a fighting force, and Agricola marched on to occupy Anglesey, which he had first seen as a young man on Suetonius' staff seventeen years before. Such fighting men as remained in the island or had escaped to it, expected that the water barrier would at least give them a respite; but Agricola, confident in the moral effect of his late victory, sent his almost amphibious Netherlands auxiliaries, horse and foot, straight in, to swim the narrows with their weapons and wooden shields. A lodgement was won before the Britons had recovered from their surprise, and in sheer dismay the islanders surrendered.

This finished the conquest of Wales; Roman armies never again had any serious fighting there. A generation later, it was even possible to put most of the forts on a caretaker basis and move the auxiliaries to the north; though Legion II, Augusta, always remained at Caerleon, until it was moved to Kent to face the Saxons. Agricola, however, made it perfectly clear that he did not regard this as a major campaign. When reporting to Rome he did not even send the "laurelled despatches" in which it was customary to announce a victory. He affected to regard the whole episode as mere police action against a tribe already conquered. (Possibly therefore the forts around Snowdonia—Carnarvon, Conway, Tomen-y-mur—had already been established by Frontinus.) This set the troops speculating with considerable interest on what he *would* regard as a major operation.

What is mysterious about this summer is why Vespasian, of all people, had permitted this interregnum to occur between Frontinus' relinquishing his command and Agricola's taking over—an interregnum which was probably responsible for a minor disaster, and might have led to worse. It can hardly have been allowed to happen so that Agricola might stay in Rome for Julia's wedding. It seems probable, though we are not told, that Frontinus must have fallen sick (though if so he made a good recovery; he long outlived Agricola), and that Agricola was sent out in a hurry half a year before it had originally been intended.

Winter was now approaching, and Agricola threw himself into the work of overhauling the civil administration —a side of his work to which a provincial governor with a war on his hands must devote himself during the winter, if at all. Knowing the British character, as Tacitus says, and having learned through the experience of former governors that force could effect little if followed by injustice, he set himself to get rid of the causes of war.

High among these stood abuses in connection with levies in cash or kind, especially grain, for the use of the army. The governor had the right to deal with these, it appears, presumably as being an army matter; but a good understanding with the financial service must have been necessary also, if a departmental wrangle was not to develop over questions of exactly what was the finance officer's business and what the army's. Some camp-commandants and their senior centurions, it transpires, had been parties to a highly profitable racket. Centurions would deliberately go out to requisition corn at a time when the destined victims had no corn to spare and the army had. There would be demands, threats, terror, and then a happy solution—happier for the Roman officials than for the villagers. The army would find the corn, would sell it to the tribe, and would then accept it back in fulfilment of the requisition. The corn was never physically moved at all, but remained all the time in the granaries; and the money paid by the Britons went into the pockets of the officials. Or alternatively, a tribe close to one of the legionary cantonments would be ordered to deliver its quota half-way across Britain to a different legion. The exact method of making a profit on this arrangement is not explained. Possibly it was a way of taking revenge on stiff-necked

communities; but no doubt also the administration would
be delighted to make arrangements, more convenient for
the tax-payers, in return for a suitable cash consideration
to the appropriate official.

It is a distressing thought that this sort of thing was apparently common in Britain under so good a governor as
Frontinus. It is generally agreed that the worse forms of
misgovernment were less rife under the Roman empire
than under the appalling republic; but if this sort of thing
could go on in half-conquered Britain under Frontinus or
Cerialis, one ceases to wonder that in the older provinces
the Roman Peace ended in impoverishment and depopulation. On these and other abuses Agricola came down
heavily, straight away, in his first winter as governor. He
had a great advantage in knowing the province; among
the hundreds of Roman administrators and generals whose
careers are known to us from tombstones and memorial
tablets, there is not one who returned three times to one
province as he did. Contacts dating from his earlier days
must have helped him greatly in his laudable aspiration to
"know everything" about what was going on.

But he was not anxious to be cashiering or punishing
officials all the time; that could only lead to bad morale.
One of his maxims was "Better put in a man who will not
go wrong than catch one who has". The essential thing
was a strict, personal attention to appointments, which was
by no means universal in the imperial services.

That appointments were made on personal recommendations, as the result of "knowing the right people", of
patronage, was not only universal in the Roman empire; it
was not even generally thought wrong. New candidates for
promotion to senatorial rank were recommended to the
emperor by senators who knew them; the young staff
officers at legion or army headquarters were selected by
commanders-in-chief on similar recommendation; and the
same system continued all the way down the hierarchy.
Soldiers posted to headquarters were known as the
Governor's or the Legion-commander's Beneficiaries, which
shows the general attitude to such promotion; and not a
few of them owed their relatively soft and comfortable posi-

tion to a timely bakshish to a general's Greek or Levantine freedman or slave secretary. At the senatorial level, Vespasian himself was said to have owed the legionary command in Britain, in which he made his name, to a timely word spoken to the Emperor Claudius' ex-slave secretary, Narcissus, by Vespasian's mistress, Cænis, who had herself been a slave in the house of Claudius' mother.

As Vespasian's case shows, the patronage system did not necessarily lead to bad appointments. It was, indeed, not even necessarily vicious, so long as both the makers of appointments and the makers of recommendations behaved responsibly; a thing more likely to happen at the higher levels, where the consequences of a bad appointment would be more conspicuous. Among his own clerical staff, whether slaves or freedmen, Agricola suppressed the whole business severely. He knew perfectly well what could be done at the secretarial level in the way of preparing business in such a way as to influence his decisions, as well as by direct or indirect suggestions; and he made it clear that he would tolerate no attempt by slave or freedman to influence service matters. He made staff and headquarter appointments, even at the level of centurion or below (the total number was never large), personally and from the men's records, not because any individual had secured any special backing. He set his face against the system of regarding an appointment as a favour or "benefice" to be conferred in the hope of gratitude. "The best man in general", ran another of his principles, "will be the most loyal."

Having thus started by taking a firm line with his own personal staff ("which most people", says Tacitus, "find quite as difficult as ruling a province"), Agricola was in a position to offer a just and tolerable administration to tribes which submitted. It is noteworthy that during all his campaigns in the distant north, he was never called back to deal with rebellion in his rear. He had achieved this by his suppression of the abuses which "through the carelessness or impatience of his predecessors," as Tacitus puts it, had rendered the Roman peace "no less terrible than war".

Relations must often have been chilly between the new commander-in-chief and some of his subordinates during that first year; but the battle was won, and quickly. Henceforward Agricola was able to follow his principle of setting himself to know everything that went on, but not to follow up everything. With minor offenders he was often satisfied with a dressing-down and a promise not to do it again. He had developed or cultivated a formidable "orderly room" manner. Like many quiet men, when he did blow up he did so with extreme violence, and no one who had experienced one of his reprimands wanted to hear another, at any rate from in front. However, people used to tell each other by way of comfort, when you had been up before the general, you knew the worst; there was at least no ground for fearing that he was keeping anything back.

There were other constructive activities on foot during this winter, of which we know from archæology. Chester, where tombstones show that Legion II, Adiutrix, spent most of its winters in Britain, was being built up as a permanent fortress. The only known inscription which names Agricola is from Chester, and bears the date "Ninth Consulship of Vespasian and Seventh of Titus"; the year 79, during the summer of which Vespasian died. It is an unusual kind of inscription, being in fact on a length of lead pipe for a water-main. Agricola was encouraging his troops to supply themselves with the amenities.

A small fragment also remains at Chester of an inscription on Purbeck marble—not local stone—and in large, very fine lettering, of the early empire, which probably ran across the face of an important building. It consists of the top part of the three letters D O M followed by what looks like the top serif of an I; and in the line above, the bottom parts of O C A, the A being represented only by its left foot. The fragment

O C A
D O M I

might well seem too small to be informative, and the museum guide says that it "has not yet yielded to interpretation". But there are possibilities.

Without claiming absolute certainty, I would suggest the following:

The fragment is *not* part of a tombstone or a private

dedication; the lettering is too large and the material too costly for anything but an official inscription. But we have hundreds of these from different parts of the empire, recording the construction of every kind of public building or works, and they always follow certain definite forms. Thus from a few letters—if they are the right letters—it is often possible to restore much; just as we can "restore" the rest if we can read no more than the letters VIC on a worn modern penny. Official Roman building inscriptions begin with the official style and honours of the reigning emperor and his heirs if any, and end, usually in smaller letters, with the names of the governor, officer and unit (or, in a civil area, the civil authority) who did and supervised the work. From the size of these letters, they should be part of the imperial style and titles; but not part of DOMINVS NOSTER, Our Lord, which is common under the later emperors, for inscriptions of that date can always be distinguished by their inferior lettering. But among all the names and titles of all the first- or second-century Cæsars, the syllable DOM forms part only of the name DOMITIANVS, the younger son of Vespasian.

But further, this is not Domitian regnant, or his name would be in the top line with nothing above. Nor is it during the reign of Titus. The letters O C A probably belong to the words TITO CÆSARI, To Titus Cæsar (the words on the inscriptions are not spaced, but separated by punctuating dots at the height of half the letter). But again, this is probably not Titus regnant, or his list of titles and appointments would take up more than one line. Even in the lifetime of his father, the line would have to be a long one. But enough inscriptions exist in honour of *Vespasian and his sons* to make it clear that into one of their normal formulæ our fragment would fit.

Before midsummer 79, then, this great slab of marble, probably about 14 feet long, was set up to celebrate the completion of a building. It probably ran across the facade, above a pillared entrance, at the point where, since the main streets of Chester still follow roughly those of the Roman camp, modern traffic still zigzags to go round the Roman headquarters.

Chapter Ten

The Advance to the North

AS the spring of 79 approached, Agricola and his legion-commanders were completing their plans for the great sweep northwards. "When summer came", says Tacitus, "and the army was concentrated, he was present everywhere on the line of march, complimenting good discipline, checking stragglers. He personally selected camp-sites, he personally reconnoitred estuaries and forests"—the places where ambushes might most easily be laid. "Meanwhile", continues the narrative, "he gave the enemy no rest from the raids of his flying columns, and then, when he had sufficiently terrorised them, he would pardon their resistance [!] and hold before their eyes the attractions of peace. Under these inducements many states, which had hitherto treated [with the empire] on equal terms, gave hostages, laid aside their hostility, and were encircled with forts; and this was done so carefully and methodically that no new part of Britain was ever won over after so little harrying."

The references to march-discipline and personal reconnaissance are, it must be confessed, part of the current picture of a good commander—they turn up again, as Birley has pointed out, in Statius' poetical account of the mild Bolanus. Like only too much in Roman and late Greek historical writing, as well as in modern journalism, they are part of the convention. However, this need not mean that they are untrue of Agricola. The reference to estuaries suggests that Agricola advanced by the west coast route, and that North Lancashire, Westmorland and Cumberland were among the areas, raided in earlier years, which were now finally taken in and consolidated. The western route is, after all, the shortest route to mid-Scotland—Edinburgh is farther west than Carlisle—and the Romans already knew the outlines of the geography of this region. Pliny, writing about the year 72, mentions the Caledonian Forest, i.e. the central Highlands, as marking the limit, not of occupation but of knowledge. If so, Agricola, like Cerialis, shows a very human preference for operating, probably with his own old legion, in a region of which he already knew something personally.

Meanwhile, Legion IX would naturally advance, keeping pace so far as possible, on the east side of the Pennines, using Cerialis' road as far as Catterick, and planting a new fort to guard the Tyne crossing at Corbridge. II, Augusta, probably remained in the south to watch the recently subdued Silures; II, Adiutrix, from Chester, and XX, his own old division, probably accompanied Agricola. Contact was made with the eastern column as opportunity offered. The Stanegate, south of the later wall of Hadrian, was one of Agricola's lateral roads; and a tile with the stamp of Legion IX shows that at some period troops of that legion were brought over to Carlisle. But during considerable periods the G.O.C. IXth Legion was necessarily left to his own resources. There was need of a good officer to command the eastern column, as Agricola himself had commanded the western force under Cerialis.

As it happens, by the chances of preservation and discovery of inscriptions, we know a good deal about this officer—one of the "new men" discovered and promoted by Vespasian. His family, the Caristanii, a name otherwise almost unknown, had been settled since the days of Augustus in the Roman colony of Antioch in Pisidia, in south-eastern Asia Minor; like Agricola, therefore, they were probably descended from a Cæsarian soldier of the revolutionary wars. They had prospered and qualified for the equestrian property-class. Gaius Caristanius Fronto, born at Antioch, had commanded, as a young man, the Bosporus Horse, a cavalry regiment recruited among the semi-civilised peoples of the Crimea, and stationed, at one time, on the Euphrates frontier, near Europos. It is thus probable that he first attracted Vespasian's notice during the

97

Jewish campaign, and that his horsemen were among the troops who marched to Europe in Vespasian's interest; the regiment next turns up on the Danube. Caristanius was among the new senators created perhaps in 70, and later promoted to prætorian rank, i.e. qualified to command a legion without going through the formalities of election to the old republican offices.

Another inscription at Antioch, broken unfortunately, gave when perfect the name of Caristanius' wife; it ends with ". . . gia Paula, daughter of Lucius". The likeliest family name is Sergia, and this is made more likely by the presence at Antioch, as shown by another broken inscription, of a man calling himself Lucius Sergius Paulus *filius* —*fils*, or junior—in order not to be confused with a well-known and like-named father.

But the well-known L. Sergius Paulus of that time and region was a man whose name is still well known today— that is, the proconsul of Cyprus who listened to the preaching of his namesake Paul of Tarsus at Paphos in the year 47. His family also had property round Antioch in Pisidia. It was probably, therefore, his son who became friendly with the Caristanii, and thus that the young Caristanius Fronto made his brilliant marriage with the daughter or granddaughter of a proconsul.

This, then, was the already experienced officer who commanded the IXth Legion on the eastern road while Agricola was in Cumberland, and who under Agricola's direction probably founded the great fort of Newstead on Tweed—Trimontium, under the "Three Peaks" of the Eildon Hills—which, repeatedly lost and reoccupied, was to be one of the chief Roman strongholds in southern Scotland for over a hundred years.

How far they penetrated during this first northern campaign we cannot say; but since they raided as far as the Tay in the following year (see the argument on page 103), they probably marched far into Scotland. The "many states" which were annexed and cut off by forts and military roads may include some small tribes which had enjoyed a brief independence since Cerialis' breaking up of the Brigantian confederacy, such as the Textoverdi in north-east England, known only from a single inscription There may well have been a similar small tribe in Cumberland; but "many states", even with an ample allowance for Roman hyperbole, must surely include the tribes of southern Scotland: the Selgovæ of the uplands, whose name survives in Selkirk, and the Otadini or Uotadini of the east coast, to whom Ptolemy assigns two "towns", apparently in Northumberland. Northward, their territory (the Manau Guotodin of the Welsh bards) extended to the Forth. These neighbours of the Brigantes perhaps came over the more easily for the same reason as the Dobunni and Cornovii a generation before, feeling that the Romans, having smitten the Brigantes, evidently had the right ideas.

For the character of British society, it is worth noting that throughout the north, from Derbyshire to Inverness, a similar pattern of tribes is three times repeated: a large tribe—but no doubt the population was thinly spread—occupies thousands of square miles of the inland hill-country, and is flanked by smaller units, corresponding to different ways of life, in the coastal lowlands. The Brigantes are flanked on the east by the chariot-driving Parisi and on the west by the Setantii, a folk known only from a place-name, "Port of the Setantii"—the predecessor of Liverpool. This is the tribe from which the Irish hero Setanta, surnamed Cuchullin, whose descent was from the larger island, appears to have been derived. Then came the Selgovæ, flanked by the Novantæ of Galloway and the Uotadini; and finally, after the mining tribe of the Damnonii in the narrow "waist" of Scotland, the great confederacy of the Caledonians in the Central Highlands, flanked in like manner by smaller tribal units in Fife, Angus, and Buchan and among the islands and promontories of the western sea-lochs.

It must have been still up at the front during the long days of a northern July that Agricola received an urgent despatch addressed to him personally. He could guess what it was before he broke the seals; Vespasian was dead. As Agricola had no doubt heard, he had been taken ill in the early summer, and putting off a journey to the south had

AGRICOLA

retired, as he often did in the hot weather, to the hill farm of his fathers at Reate. There he continued relentlessly to transact state business from his bed and, when fevered, to drink very cold water in quantities which his doctors, who could of course do nothing with him, considered unwise. "I fancy I am becoming a god," he said, alluding to the deification of deceased emperors; but he still worked and still drank his cold water. On June 23rd, weak with dysentery, he was lying exhausted; but with a flash of his old spirit he suddenly said: "A generalissimo ought to die standing"; and with that he rose to his feet and died accordingly.

Agricola paraded the troops, and they took the oath of allegiance, and cheered "Titus Imperator". Afterwards he sat down to draft a suitable loyal message on behalf of the army, to go by the returning despatch rider. He knew Titus quite well, of course, but everyone always found the precise mixture of condolence with joy in the new reign rather hard to hit off. . . . Anyhow, there would be no trouble about the succession this time; Titus had been all but co-Emperor for years. But the whole Roman world could not but feel that a master hand had relaxed its grasp of the reins.

Before the summer was over there was more news from Italy—news horrific and catastrophic. There had been many earth tremors lately round the Bay of Naples; but no one was prepared for what happened on the 24th August. The whole top of Vesuvius blew off, in the most famous if not the most violent volcanic eruption in history, overwhelming two towns: the vulgar little seaside resort of Pompeii and the more opulent and cultivated Herculaneum. Among the dead was Pliny the encyclopædist, commanding the home fleet in the bay, who, having taken a squadron over, both to save life and to observe the phenomena in a spirit of scientific curiosity, was overcome by poisonous fumes. The eruption owes much of its fame to two letters which his nephew and adopted son, Pliny the Younger, wrote years afterwards to Tacitus, then collecting materials for his *Histories*.

Leaving Caristanius at York to keep an eye on the Brigantes, Agricola went south for the winter, to meet Domitia, who had joined him in Britain, and to attend to civil business. Having effectively purged the administration in the previous year, he was able to throw himself into a project which he had much at heart: the furtherance of Romanisation, as he had seen it in Aquitaine.

Agricola was certainly not the sole parent of Romanisation in Britain, as one might gather from Tacitus; but there is no reason to deny him credit for his enthusiastic work for it. There were already British families possessing Roman citizenship with the name of Claudius, whose citizenship dates therefore from the reign of Claudius or of his adopted son, Claudius Nero; and a fragment of a building-inscription from Bath, Aquæ Sulis, already a spa of some note, bears the date "Seventh consulship of the Emperor Vespasian"; A.D. 76, in the time of Frontinus. But the time was ripe now for assimilation to proceed with a faster tempo. The south was thoroughly at peace by now; there was never another rebellion south of Derbyshire, though many north of it; Roman soldiers were seldom seen, except for drafts, or the governor's guard, or a squad seconded for the protection of tax-gatherers or of bullion in transit. Local government was in the hands of the local chiefs, organised, as in Gaul, into Roman-style municipal corporations, co-opting their sons and nephews to fill vacancies, and managing their own districts, subject to paying their taxes and the grain-levy and to the reference of capital charges to the governor's court.

Agricola must have travelled indefatigably, using all his influence, and the prestige and popularity that he had earned, in the cause of civilisation. One wonders how much his wife travelled with him, and whether she liked it. "He encouraged individuals, he assisted communities [e.g. by the loan of army surveyors, architects and craftsmen] to build themselves temples, town-centres, private houses. He praised the willing, he censured the unresponsive; and so competition to win favour took the place of compulsion. Now, too, he encouraged the literary education of chieftains' sons, and used to express his conviction of the superiority of the British native intelligence over the studied eloquence of the Gauls, with the result that people who had but lately refused to speak Latin were now eager to be eloquent in it. The Roman dress, too, gained in prestige; the toga was much in evidence; and gradually the Britons drifted into the demoralising pleasures of [lounging in] porticoes and bath-establishments and giving elegant dinner-parties. This the unsuspecting natives called civilisation, when it was merely one way of holding them down."

That Agricola himself took such a cynical view of it all does not, of course, necessarily follow.

The fostering of Romanisation continued, naturally, to occupy Agricola during subsequent winters; as did also the business of descending heavily upon any recrudescence of the earlier racketeering. It is appropriate, however, to mention the beginning of his culture-drive, in chronological order, as Tacitus does, between campaigns.

Summer of the year 80 saw Agricola in the field again. He had to take leave of Caristanius, who was promoted by Titus to the government of Pamphylia, in his native Asia Minor. However, he was now in country where lateral communication was less difficult. By routes which recent work has shown Agricola's army to have used—south-west from Trimontium by Ettrick to Annandale, with forts at Oakwood and Raeburnfoot; west up the Tweed to the wide levels about the upper Clyde, near Carstairs—it was now easier to keep in touch with both columns. The fort of Castledykes, near Carstairs, it is tempting to suggest, might be the Roman Maromagus, "Wide Plain" in Celtic, three marches from Trimontium. Between them lay Dubabissis, "Dark Water", perhaps the fort of Lyne, where the Tweed runs dark in its deep valley, and a place which we have already mentioned, Venutio.

Tacitus continues: "The third year's campaign opened up new peoples, the tribes being harried as far as the Tanaus estuary. The terrified enemy did not dare to attack the army, even when battered by particularly severe storms, and there was time for fort-building as well. Experts noted that no commander had ever had a better eye for a position. No fort planted by Agricola was ever either taken by storm or evacuated by its garrison under truce." This point at least in Tacitus' encomium is confirmed by the best possible independent testimony. Sixty years later, when the Romans in greater force campaigned once more over the same ground, practically every site chosen by Agricola was used again. But a question which requires attention is how far he penetrated in this third campaign.

The correct answer to this turns upon what Tacitus says about the *fourth* campaign, that of 81: "The fourth summer was occupied in securing the ground which he had overrun"; and a leading feature of this consolidation was the building of a line of forts on the Forth–Clyde line. Tacitus does *not* say, though curiously many modern scholars do—even good scholars—that in his fourth campaign Agricola *advanced* to the Forth–Clyde line *and* fortified it; he says quite explicitly, in the above words, that in this campaign no farther advance was made. The Tanaus estuary was therefore certainly not the navigable mouth of the Tyne; and much less the North Tyne in East Lothian, which could not by any stretch be called an estuary. As Richmond has put it, if a general, after raiding up to A, consolidates on the line B–C, A is beyond the line B–C. Moreover, we find that though all the four known manuscripts of the biography (which are frequently corrupt) give the name "Tanaus", three, including the two best and earliest, have also a correction "Taus". The estuary up to which Agricola raided in that wet and windy summer was, in short, the Tay.

The name Tanaus *may*, no doubt, have been the ancient name of one of the Tynes; if so, its insertion here is a slip of the pen by Tacitus. But since we have the correction "Taus" in our manuscripts, it is much likelier that the corruption started with a scribe copying the text. This is the likelier, since the name Tana*is* was a river-name famous in the ancient world as a synonym for the ends of the earth: the name of the Russian Don.

It is all the likelier that Agricola pushed his advance in 80 as far as the Tay, because it seems from Ptolemy's *Geography* that the Firth of Tay and the River Earn, which runs into it, formed the northern boundaries of the tribes of mid-Scotland. Chief of these were the Damnonii of the Forth and Clyde valleys, whose name is cognate with that of the Dumnonii of Devon and the Fir-Domnann of Irish mythology, explained by scholars of early Ireland as "deep diggers in the earth": in short, a mining people. The appearance of the name in three widely separated regions on the shores of the Irish Sea must be a legacy of those sea-borne movements, already ancient in Agricola's time, which spread elements of a common culture, known to us chiefly from its burials, along the western seaboard of Europe and the British Isles. East of the Damnonii lay the Venicônes, probably in Fife; a small tribe, with rich soil, in an isolated position, and exposed by sea. They made peace quickly, and avoided intensive Roman occupation.

In 81, then, the advance halted to consolidate on and behind the Forth–Clyde line; an operation on which Tacitus comments in somewhat curious terms:

"The fourth summer was occupied in securing the ground overrun; and if the valour of the armies and the prestige of the name of Rome had permitted it, a boundary had been found in Britain itself. For the Clyde and Forth, tidal river-mouths running far inland from opposite seas, are divided only by a narrow tract of land. This was now strongly garrisoned, and the whole nearer extent of the country secured, while the enemy were banished as though into another island."

At no less than nine sites on the isthmus the traces of Agricola's operations have, in fact, been detected. The ditches of his actual forts underlie those of the later Romans at Mumrills (near Falkirk), Croy Hill, Bar Hill and Old Kilpatrick on the Clyde; Camelon, just north of the later wall, is his; and pottery of his period, or circumstantial evidence, points to the presence of his troops also at Rough Castle, Castlecary and Westerwood in the right-central sector, and at Cadder overlooking the Kelvin. (Every one of these sites was reoccupied sixty years later.)

But what is the significance of the expression "if the prestige of the name of Rome had permitted it", etc.? It is evident that there must have been discussion of the question whether it would not be best to halt here and avoid the cost of further campaigns, and especially of the numerous additional auxiliary units that would be required if the whole of Scotland were to be garrisoned. Against halting at the isthmus there were two arguments: that of prestige, here mentioned, and the argument, very familiar to the Romans, that the existence of kindred and neighbouring tribes in a state of freedom outside the empire set a bad example and was productive of unrest among recently conquered peoples inside it; an argument which Agricola himself used later in favour of extending the conquest to Ireland as well.

There was another fact that must have been present to Agricola's mind during this summer. It was his fourth in Britain. Cerialis had been here for three years only; Frontinus for four at most. It would not be surprising if the Emperor were to inform him that his successor had been appointed. No doubt if, after his achievements, he had given any hint that he would be glad of relief, Titus would have obliged him. But there can be no doubt, either, that Agricola did not desire relief. He was, Tacitus says, by nature an optimist. Also he genuinely loved Britain, even if it was, in part, with the love of a hunter for his quarry. He was sure that, given plenty of troops and a free hand, the conquest could be completed in, say, another couple of years. Would he be allowed to do it?

The view that the Forth–Clyde line should be a permanent frontier was certainly not, then, Agricola's view. Therefore, if Tacitus mentions it, it can only be because it was the view held in some quarters in Rome; the view of some people, at least, whom Tacitus respected or whom he could not ignore. Much in the tone of his biography, it has often been recognised, becomes easier to understand if it is taken to be in part an apologia for one who ended by becoming a somewhat controversial figure.

Agricola did in the end, as the world knows, get three more years in the British command; and he got permission to go ahead, in spite of the fact that there was trouble on the Rhine and few troops to spare. But he got it, not finally from the experienced soldier and administrator Titus, but from his brother and successor, twelve years younger, who had been deliberately kept in the background by Vespasian to avoid rivalry, and who had not been expected to succeed to the throne, at least for many years.

For on the 14th of September, 81, in his forty-second year, the good-natured Titus died. Domitian was acclaimed *Imperator* by the household troops, and succeeded to the throne three weeks before his thirtieth birthday, proud, nervous, intelligent, full of inferiority complex, little trained, and thirsting for such military glory as had been won by his father and brother. There was far more in him than is admitted by the conventional portrait of him as a sadistic tyrant, though there was something of that, too. Nevertheless, it was a bad day for Rome, for Domitian himself and for many of his subjects when Titus died of an autumn fever and when Domitian came to supreme power so suddenly and so unready.

Chapter Eleven

Winter in the North

BY the time Agricola heard the news this time, the army must have been moving towards its winter quarters. Its main force, indeed, had probably never been concentrated, since there had been no major advance this year. In the circumstances, the business of swearing-in and securing the acclamation of the troops, especially the citizen legions, would have to be done through the legion-commanders. The governor himself could take the place of honour this time in loyal ceremonies at some of the chief civil centres: the ex-soldier colony of Colchester, tribal capitals like Verulam, and trading centres like the great sprawling settlement of London, whose corporate status at this time is uncertain.

At the earliest opportunity, too, he would naturally draft another suitably complimentary message of enthusiasm, loyalty and condolence on the death of his brother to the young emperor: Generalissimo Cæsar Domitianus Augustus. His feelings about the change, like those of most senators, must have been mixed. Domitian's chief hour of glory hitherto had been in the winter of 69–70, during the revolution, while his father and elder brother were still in the east; and he had shown such eagerness in grasping at power on that occasion that old Vespasian, reading, at Alexandria, a long list of new appointments, said dryly: "I'm surprised that he hasn't superseded *me* so far." At the same time, Agricola's most personal interest just then must have been in the question whether, from the new Chief, he could obtain an extension of his command and permission to cross the Forth and complete the conquest of Britain.

While correspondence on this subject between Agricola

and Rome, and no doubt also discussion of the British question at Rome itself, continued at the highest level, winter closed down over the hill-forts in Wales, in the Brigantian country and north to the Forth–Clyde line, where isolated auxiliary cohorts had the task of maintaining, for the next six months, Rome's hold on the recently conquered ground.

In the second century, after Hadrian's Wall was built and when cohorts often remained in the same forts for many years at a time, we know from their building inscriptions and religious dedications what units garrisoned many positions; while statue-bases and tombstones, both in Britain and elsewhere, tell us the names and sometimes the careers of many officers who served here, and of not a few of the rank and file. For these early days inscriptions are scanty; but one prefect of Agricola's forces on the Forth–Clyde line can be named, and may stand for all of them: Lucius Tanicius Verus—*if*, that is, he is identical with a centurion of that name (the family name is a very rare one), born at Vienne on the Rhône, who was serving in Egypt in Legion III, Cyrenaica, in 80–81. Transfers from the army in Egypt to those in the west seem to have been rare. On the other hand one might add, in favour of identifying the authors of two inscriptions, the fact that the practice of setting up inscriptions seems to have been habit-forming, like that of writing to *The Times*. Out of our not many scores of inscriptions from Roman Scotland, no less than four are dedications by one centurion, three by another, and an eighth by a man also known from an inscription on Hadrian's Wall.

Near Tanicius' post in Egypt there was a broken colossus of a Pharaoh, identified by Greeks and Romans as Memnon, Son of the Dawn, the King of the East who, in post-Homeric saga, tried to relieve Troy and was killed there. When the broken stone-work expanded in the sun at dawn, after contracting in the chill desert night, the statue often emitted a clear musical twang. It was a curiosity much visited by Greek and Roman tourists. Tanicius "heard Memnon" over a dozen times between November, A.D. 80, and June, 81. He made notes of the dates and had them recorded on stone before leaving the district, for the edification of such as should come after.

From centurion in a legion to prefect of auxiliary infantry was quite possible promotion for a man of some education, such as Tanicius was; and no doubt Tanicius was delighted when the news of it came through. He was probably somewhat taken aback when he found out that his transfer was to be from Egypt in June, when he last records hearing Memnon, to mid-Scotland for the winter; but that, of course, was typical of a side of army life sometimes hypostatised as the Practical Joke Department. If it is the same man, and not, say, a hypothetical second-century grandson, Tanicius probably went straight from the River Nile to the River Kelvin in the autumn of 81; for the occupation of Agricola's forts on the isthmus was very brief, perhaps lasting only till the renewal of the advance, early in 83.

Tanicius found himself in charge of a fort on the brow of a hill at Cadder, near where his inscription was seen by Camden, a place now some five miles from the centre of Glasgow. The Romano-British name of the place may have been Volitanium, meaning something like "The Plateau". There was a good field of vision over a wide valley (the Kelvin) to higher ground beyond; and beyond that again rose the great, rounded, boggy mass of the Campsie Fells. Farther still, down a wide valley on the left of those hills, one could catch a glimpse of real mountain country twenty miles away, at least when the weather was clear enough; but that seemed to be seldom. Beyond those hills was the land of the Caledonians.

The chief disadvantage about the view over the valley was that much of it was choked with a thick growth of birch and hazel thickets, in which any number of enemies might have lurked. Certainly anyone who did lurk down there might seem to be inviting pneumonia or rheumatism, but the local savages were said to be so tough that they did not suffer. It was believed by the Roman army at a later date, if not already, that they could last out for days bodily under water.

Anyhow, this was where he would be spending the

winter, with half-a-dozen centurions under him, a sprink-
ling of old soldiers and junior n.c.o.s, and four-hundred-
odd young savages of his own from the Low Countries or
Central Europe. It was going to be tough, and much would
depend on keeping morale right by constant training and
patrolling (if the enemy did not keep them busy enough),
and by having things as trim, warm, dry and comfortable
as might be in the hutted lines where the men slept. In the
meantime, he vowed an altar to Silvanus, the primitive
Roman god of all wild country, if he lived till the
spring.

As the autumn came on, all units worked hard at fortification (priority I), securing their supplies and getting a
solid roof over their heads: tiles for preference. Tiles
meant a lot of carrying, unless there was an army tilery
handy, but, on the other hand, they could not be set on
fire. If it had to be thatch, one was grateful for the wet
climate. Large tanks for surface water were also dug, in
case the palisades on top of the earthen entrenchments
were fired. Long convoys of sulky natives came in with
corn (their own corn) until, by Agricola's express orders,
every fort had enough for a year. It was stored carefully in
granaries with floors raised off the ground on little pillars,
against rats and damp. Hutments for the troops were of
wood, but if it was possible to build a stone granary, so
much the better.

Outside, the relentless centurions superintended the
digging of a second ditch, and a third, and even a fourth
and fifth, especially on exposed sides. They were often
probably filled with cut thorn-bushes, or the inner sides
protected with *abattis* of medium-sized felled trees, lashed
together with their branches pointing towards the enemy.
The necessary clearance of all bushes and other cover from
a wide space round the fort would supply plenty of
material. There were other kinds of booby-traps, too. In
suitable soil, a whole area of ground might be honey-
combed with small, deep pits, each row covering the gaps
in the row before it, and each pit holding a sharpened
stake. Masked with brushwood, they could be very effective against anyone trying either to approach stealthily by

night or to charge by daylight. The troops called them
"lilies"—arum lilies. A set of them, probably dug that
very winter, may still be seen in the eastern sector of the
isthmus, at the Roman fort of Rough Castle. It was thus
that "pottes", such as Robert Bruce once purposed to use,
were first introduced into Scotland.

The days shortened, and the army settled in for the
winter. The legionary detachments finished off the sections
of military road which they had been laying (they were
the engineers of the army as well as the "armour"), and
withdrew to their relatively comfortable cantonments. The
nights were cold and dark, the days, what there was of
them, dark and foggy; Tanicius must have regretted the
clear skies of Egypt. Less often, it was colder still, with a
crackle of frost in the morning and clear days when one
could see down Strath Blane to the mountains of the Caledonians, with the silver head of Ben Lomond bright
against the pale northern blue.

The forts on the isthmus, which were only a few miles
apart, kept in touch with each other by signals from their
towers and by armed parties; by large fighting patrols
when it seemed necessary. Some of the forts in the hills
farther south must have been, in practice, much more
isolated. On the Forth–Clyde line there was probably not
much danger of being actually under siege, unless the
formidable Caledonians chose voluntarily to provoke
Rome; but of that there was little sign. Things must have
been fairly bleak; the days when each battalion could
build itself a stone Turkish-bath house, where the men off
duty could crowd in, in the evenings, and sing songs and
play endless games of chance, attested by dedications to the
Goddess of Fortune beside or in the bath-houses—these
days lay still in the future, in times when the army had
finally gone over to garrison-duty in fixed positions. So did
the days when they could build a defended annexe, outside the sacred precincts of the fort proper, for their
women and children. But there was plenty of wood for
fires; and at midwinter, if things were quiet, the festival
of the Saturnalia, when people gave each other presents,
and when good-natured Romans traditionally let their

slaves play at being master, was perhaps not very unlike Christmas in the British Army.

For the rest, "winter quarters" did not mean that the Roman Army went to bed and stayed there. Tacitus says explicitly of Agricola's forts, that from them "Sorties were frequent". That meant, if a fort was besieged by a local rising, sudden and violent counter-attacks from the gates, as opportunity offered; or, when things were quiet, constant patrolling along the military roads, and also off them, limited chiefly by the mud. So the midwinter passed. The worst was not over; then as now, "as the day lengthened, the cold strengthened"; and commandants had to keep an anxious eye on their diminishing stocks of food and fuel. But there was a feeling of having turned the corner, of "counting the days" till spring, when relief could be expected. If things were bad, at least that gave a chance of distinguishing one's self. Agricola had a name for being good about mentioning in despatches any commandant or centurion who had held out in a tight corner. His subordinates appreciated it; and though at some times and places there was severe pressure on his outlying units, it remained proudly on his record that he never lost a fort.

Even to the loneliest outpost there came a day when a yell from the look-out tower told of cavalry on the skyline. Later, the square masses of a legion could be seen descending the forward slopes. Everyone cheered; and other men, no doubt, besides L. Tanicius, commissioned the best stone-cutters in their units to record, in the time-honoured phrase, that to the God of the Wilds they willingly and duly paid their vows.

Chapter Twelve

People of Roman Britain

IN the south of Britain, Romanisation was proceeding satisfactorily. The schoolmasters and professors of rhetoric must have been numbered by scores; Gauls, most of them, since they were nearest, and their bright young literary men found posts in the new oversea province relatively easy to get.

> *Eloquent Gauls have trained afar*
> *The leaders of a British bar,*
> *And Thulé, like her predecessor,*
> *Debates the hire of a professor,"*

says Juvenal forty years after. The idea of a British barrister was as funny in its day as that of cannibals in top-hats. It is, in fact, the same joke. But Juvenal's references to Britain in his satires seem to be something more than merely conventional jokes about the ends of the earth. There was, at least, a man with the same names, D. Junius Juvenalis, who dedicated an altar at Aquinum, Juvenal's native town, some time after the death of Vespasian, and who describes himself as sometime commander of the 1st Dalmatian Cohort, a regiment which was in Britain; and Juvenal the satirist, if born in 55, as a dubious tradition says, might very well have held that post under Agricola, and so seen for himself the Brigantian hill-forts, the war-chariots, the whales (then fairly common in northern waters), the mushroom Romanisation and the Gallic teachers of Latin eloquence, to which he alludes.

Some travelling professors came from farther afield and, with the prestige of knowing not only Latin but Greek, the very fountain-head of eloquence and culture, presumably commanded higher fees. Plutarch says that he met at Delphi, at the festival of 83, a literature teacher just returned from Britain, named Demetrius of Tarsus; and since, though the name Demetrius is very common in Greece, Greeks of any kind were very uncommon in Britain, it has often been suggested that he is the same Demetrius who dedicated at York two little votive tablets of silver-coated bronze, with inscriptions in Greek to the Sea-Gods and "the Gods of the Imperial Prætorium", presumably on safe arrival at his distant destination.

Here a word of caution is necessary. The dedicator of the plaque addressed to the Gods of the Imperial Prætorium calls himself Demetrius the Scribe, or Secretary; and a scribe was not the same thing as a *grammaticus,* or lecturer in literature. A *grammaticus* was either a travelling freelance, or retained and salaried as a teacher. A scribe was a clerk or secretary in private or public service, usually a slave or freedman; an individual of humble status, though he might be handling important work. *If* Demetrius at York is Demetrius of Tarsus, then he appears to have blossomed out from secretary at the time of his arrival in Britain to lecturer before he returned home; which is, of course, perfectly possible, especially in the career of an enterprising Greek or Levantine.

Now, the Demetrius at York is not the freedman of a Roman official. He has no Roman name, and a freedman always took the name of his "patron", his former owner. But only one kind of office at York in these early days could possibly be employing a free-born Greek secretary; that is, a government office, possibly connected with the financial branch, but more probably that of the G.O.C. IXth Legion.

Demetrius must, in any case, have spent some years in Britain; it would be worth nobody's while to make the long journey from the eastern Mediterranean for less. But this takes us back to the years when Caristanius Fronto, from Antioch in Pisidia, had the command at York. If, then, the identification is sound—and good authorities have accepted it without question—then Demetrius of Tarsus was employed by Caristanius, who came from the same part of the world and may have known him in the east, as a civilian secretary; hence Demetrius' rather unusual dedication to "the Gods of the Prætorium". One wonders whether Caristanius had his lady with him at York; things were decidedly more settled by now in Britain than they had been seven years earlier; and, if so, whether, between Sergia Paula and Demetrius of Tarsus, the name of his notorious compatriot Paul of Tarsus ever arose in conversation. When Caristanius was transferred to Asia Minor, Demetrius, it seems, elected not to go back with him, but to stay in Britain and go into Cultural Relations. He appears to have prospered. When he did go home two or three years later he appears at Delphi in distinguished company, discussing the cessation of oracular inspiration with a circle including Plutarch, the friend of Roman noblemen and consuls; and before he went he was privileged to accompany, as a civilian observer, one of Agricola's exploring parties among the Western Isles of Scotland.

Such a sustained educational effort produced rapid results. Helped by the fact that Old Celtic was closely akin to Latin, Latin was soon generally understood, at least in the towns; and not only by the chieftains' families, who kept Gallic tutors and attended lectures and displays of public speaking, but by the ordinary man in the street, as many casual scribbles show us. "London: By the Temple of Isis" runs an address, scratched on the necks of two different jugs now known—and of how many which are not? There must have been a wine-shop there; and presumably one paid a deposit on the container. "Austalis has been going off on his own every day for a fortnight," says a famous scribble in broken Latin, written in the wet clay of a tile before it was fired; apparently a comment on one of his mates by a workman at the brick-works. Some fragments of business or legal documents, also from London (preserved through the fact that on a wax-covered tablet, the writing-pad of the ancient world, the steel pen has bitten through on to the wood), are less surprising. They refer to contracts, sales and the building of a ship. In one of them an oath is sworn by Jupiter and the Divinity of the Emperor Domitian, which gives a date in the years 81–96.

Scratches on pottery from the smaller towns, too, show that the process was not confined to London. At Leicester, Ratæ of the Coritani, a workman writes on an unfired tile, "Primus has made ten"; while the words, scratched in careful block capitals on a fragment of a bowl, "Verecunda the Actress; Lucius the Gladiator" look like a pathetic love-token, perhaps one of a pair exchanged by two slave entertainers who hoped to meet again. A group comes from Silchester, the county-town of the Belgic Atrebates, in Berkshire: "Satis", perhaps "stint completed", written with the finger-tip, with a sigh of relief, in the wet clay of yet another unfired tile; "Thief" on a chip of imported red "Samian" ware—an insult thrown over somebody's garden wall. Somebody else uses a sherd in order to note down a date: 26th September. A less serious spirit writes a sentence ending with the word "girl"; but only the last word survives. Finally, a set of personal names and other words on one tile, giving no connected sense, but repeating certain syllables, looks as if we have a relic of somebody's actual writing lesson:

> "Pertacus perfidus
> Campester Lucilianus
> Campanus they all fell silent".

The last words give perhaps the most famous tag in all the works of Vergil: the first words of the book containing Æneas' story of the burning of Troy.

Of one class of society only we have no written record whatever, and therefore no individual records; the foundation of all societies, the shepherds and peasants who remained on the land. They, however, outside the towns, continued to speak Old British, the parent of Welsh. We can be sure of this, not merely because Welsh is a Celtic and not a Latin language, but because, even in eastern England, on the wolds of Lincolnshire and east Yorkshire, within living memory, a set of recognisable primitive Welsh numerals was still used for counting a score of sheep.

In Roman Britain, as elsewhere, peasants and simple

folk emerge in history or in official records only when history or officialdom forcibly impinges upon them. The Briton who remained on the land wrote nothing; he did not even have a headstone to his grave. We do know the names of a considerable number of ordinary Britons, and sometimes something of their life-history; but as a rule it is only because they were drafted into the Roman army and shipped off abroad. Lucco the son of Trenus, of the Gloucestershire Dobunni, was enlisted during Agricola's time, in A.D. 79, and served on the Danube in the First British Cohort, 1,000 strong. There he married a local girl named Tutula, of the tribe of the Azali, and they had a boy and two girls, not counting any babies who died. Later the regiment served beyond the Danube, in Dacia, in the wars which ended with the Emperor Trajan annexing that country, including the Transylvanian gold-mines. It distinguished itself in action, and was rewarded with the title of "Roman Citizens". Lucco survived the hazards and hardships of twenty-five years' service, and was granted his discharge on the eve of the last Dacian War, on the 12th January 105. The regiment stayed on in Dacia as part of the garrison; but Lucco seems to have settled down with his gratuity in his wife's country, now western Hungary. It was there that his certificate of honourable discharge with citizenship for his family, inscribed on the usual bronze plaque, was found in recent years, and acquired by the National Museum at Buda-Pest.

The British regiments in general, it is gratifying to find, seem to have been highly appreciated in the Roman army. The First Britons, another double-sized cohort (not the same as the First British, and no doubt fierce rivals), gained, in the same series of Danubian wars, a quite unrivalled series of honours: Trajan's Own, Decorated for Valour, Loyal and True, Roman Citizens. The whole string of titles is proudly flaunted in a bronze certificate of unusual form, recording the grant of citizenship to the whole battalion "on the field" in Dacia in August 106, and issued to Marcus Ulpius Novantico, son of Adcobrovatus, from Leicester. Other regiments appear with a selection of the same titles or with different ones: the Second Britons, Em-

peror Nerva's Own, Roman Citizens, for example; or
Domitian's Own First British Cavalry, Roman Citizens.
This regiment was also among those specially transferred
by Trajan to the east for his war with Parthia.

Among the troops depicted in the battle-scenes on
Trajan's Column, which was that Emperor's monument for
his conquest of Dacia, there figure some very rough-
looking fellows, much wilder than the normal Roman
auxiliaries. They are dressed in Celtic trousers; they are
naked to the waist, which was a Celtic fashion in battle;
and they brandish, as their favourite weapon, what British
troops of World War I first entitled a "cosh". Some have
suggested that they are German allies; but in view of the
distinguished part played by the Britons in these wars, one
would expect them to find some place on the monument;
and it is at least tempting to suggest that Trajan's war-
artist has here represented the fierce "native infantry"
from Rome's newest province.

If some Britons serving in the Roman army married on
the Continent, some soldiers of the Roman army in Britain
married British girls. With no colour-bar and with the
spread of Latin swiftly demolishing the language-barrier,
the Roman empire was indeed a "melting-pot" of peoples
only to be matched by the United States. We have the
tombstone in North Africa of a centurion, Flavius Virilis,
long after Agricola's time, who while serving in Britain
had married a woman named Bodicca—the same name as
that of Queen Boudicca; it means, by the way, Victoria.
And while Agricola was still living there was another
British girl, named Claudia Rufina, or Red-Head, married
to a man of good standing in Rome. Claudia's family name
shows that she came of a Romanised family; she was perhaps a granddaughter of one of the chiefs enfranchised by
Claudius. Still, she was indubitably descended from quite
recent ancestors who used to paint themselves blue. The
poet Martial himself says so, in a poem in which he con-
gratulates Rufina at once on her beautiful Greco-Roman
manners and on the birth of her third child.

In every direction the Roman army, and the civil service
also, mingled the races and unified the culture, though at

118

a dull and "mass-produced" level, of Europe and the Mediterranean. The tombstone of yet another centurion who had served in Britain in the first century was discovered in 1938 in Palestine: that of Tiberius Claudius Fatalis, son of Tiberius, born at Rome; centurion successively in Legions II Augusta, XX Victrix, II Augusta (again), XI Claudia and XIV Gemina Martia Victrix (both in Central Europe), and finally in XII Fulminata (the "Thundering Legion") and X (once the favourite legion of the great Cæsar), both in the eastern army group. While serving in the Xth, Fatalis died in Palestine, aged forty-two, either during the Jewish War or on garrison duty thereafter, and was buried by his freedwoman Iónicé, a Greek-named slave-girl whom he had bought, married, liberated, and left as his heir, with the twin formulæ of Roman gravestones: Quiet rest thy bones, and light lie the earth upon thee. Fatalis himself was perhaps the son of a freedman; for his birthplace, Rome, and his father's names, the imperial names Tiberius Claudius, look as if that father had been one of the slave and ex-slave clerks and secretaries of the Claudian civil service.

British Lucco and his Danubian Tutula, Virilis and Bodicca, British Rufina and her Roman husband, Fatalis and his Greek Iónicé—they are four examples among many hundreds on record, of the way in which the empire mingled the peoples of Europe and the near East, producing, in spite of subsequent barbarian invasions, more kinship by blood among the peoples of all these regions than is often realised today.

While Roman soldiers of all nations served in their garrisons and laid their roads and married locally, and while Britons struggled at their writing-lessons and learned to read Vergil and to drape the difficult toga round them as befitted a Roman gentleman, the governor worked on, still constantly travelling, encouraging building projects, cutting knots in the administration and dealing with the heavy correspondence that followed him from place to place. There would be a good deal of routine correspondence with his legion-commanders and other officers; a good deal with the finance officer, necessary if relations of the two services were to remain as friendly as Agricola liked them to be; a good deal with fellow-senators in Italy, requiring commissions for their invariably blameless and promising sons and nephews and friends' sons; and a good deal with British chiefs and local authorities, arising out of business initiated on his last visit or to be settled on his next. Partly as a matter of flattery and partly from real need, his presence must have been constantly in demand simultaneously in different corners of the province. But the most important correspondence, and that requiring the greatest care and closest attention, was of course that, both on important details and on high policy, with the emperor in Rome.

About all this side of Agricola's work we have no direct evidence; but for what official correspondence could be like, and for the range of routine business involved, we are fortunate enough actually to possess a file of original correspondence of the next generation; the letters exchanged between the younger Pliny as governor of Bithynia in Asia Minor, and the Emperor Trajan. The business transacted includes questions arising out of litigation and local feuds; building projects and their cost, the relations to be observed between Roman law and local custom; the validity of decrees of an emperor who had (like Nero) been officially damned; the question of licensing local voluntary societies. (Can they be trusted not to become cells of anti-imperial conspiracy?) An escaper from enemy territory is sent to Rome to tell his story. A finance official demands a military escort while tax-collecting in the mountains; the emperor agrees, but is anxious about the frittering away of military strength in little detachments. The same question arises over prison-guards, the trouble being that local slave-warders are apt to be inefficient. Pliny gives a testimonial to a minor official. Pliny has given his wife an official movement-order on urgent compassionate grounds, and hopes it is all right. ("Certainly, my dear Pliny.") There are loyal messages on New Year's Day and the Emperor's accession-day; there are enclosures and references to files.

In the middle of all this arises the question of the

Christians, who decline to revere the divinity of the Emperor. By means of a number of executions and an amnesty for the repentant, Pliny is getting congregations back to the lately deserted temples very satisfactorily. He had also decided to torture two maidservants (deaconesses?) in the hope of getting further light on the suspected enormities of the Christians; but got nothing except "a low form of superstition expressed with great volubility". It is an episode which one used to take for granted, as the kind of thing that naturally would happen "in those days"; but in later and worse times it emerges as a Gestapo story, in all its original ghastliness. Two points of interest about it are that Pliny asks what he ought to do about an anonymous letter naming a long list of alleged Christians ("Take no notice of such things whatever," replies Trajan), and that he asks for instructions on procedure, since "I have never been present at any trials of Christians". This implies something which is not always noticed: that by the early second century there had not only been trials of Christians at Rome, but enough of them for something like a regular procedure to have evolved.

The Christian question, which was almost to disrupt the empire in the third century, is not likely, however, to have troubled Agricola. In this remote western province there cannot have been many early Christians, though it would be rash, in view of the amount of coming and going, to assume that there were none. The first recorded British martyr, the soldier Albanus (St. Alban) belongs to the third or early fourth century. The problems that troubled the sleep of early governors of Britain were problems of frontier policy; the great problem of whether to stop on a given line, and how to fortify that line if one did.

Such questions could be sufficiently worrying. If misunderstandings can easily arise at opposite ends of a wireless link, between the man on the spot, who feels that London does not appreciate the force of his arguments, and a home government which feels that G.H.Q. "out there" takes too narrow a view, it can be imagined what things were like when the only links were relays of horsemen. What could happen over major decisions on frontier policy

emerges, a generation after Agricola, in connection with
Hadrian's Wall. During the four years or so in which the
Wall was in building, several major changes were made in
the original plan agreed by Hadrian on his visit to the
frontier in 122. The originally planned thickness was reduced from ten feet to eight, perhaps as an economy; and
the whole wall was made less of a police barrier and more
of a battle-line, with the counter-attack troops, horse and
foot, originally held back behind the wall, moved up into
large forts on the Wall itself, with sally-ports north of it.
All these modifications originated, no doubt, in local experience; but for all of them the British command had to
obtain the agreement of the Emperor, a very busy man.
Appeals to sanction major changes in his original decisions
can never be welcome to an overworked administrator
with many other things on his mind; and it is sad, no
doubt, but not surprising, that before the end of his career
the governor Platorius Nepos, once the intimate friend of
Hadrian, was his friend no more.

Naturally, not all Roman imperial correspondence was
of the same character. Personal and local factors would, if
we had the files, make every file different. Pliny in Bithynia
was a meticulous little Treasury expert on a special mission
to "sort" the finances of a badly misgoverned province.
Trajan was a self-confident soldier; Hadrian a feverishly
active, unresting intellectual. Agricola himself was always
very respectful to constituted authority; but his relations
with his three successive emperors must have differed
greatly. To Vespasian he was a young man who had been
promoted quickly for merit and for political reliability.
Titus was a man of his own age, easy-going, affable, and
with the self-confidence bred of wide experience in command. And now Domitian, ten years his junior—Domitian,
the unknown quantity, acutely conscious of a youth spent
sometimes in considerable squalor—was Generalissimo and
Cæsar Augustus.

Naturally Agricola sent the proper loyal and flattering
messages at the usual seasons. Naturally, too, he hoped to
obtain from the young Augustus an extension of his command, with permission to advance and complete the con-

quest. Also, the young Domitian was not yet the grim figure of the end of his reign, steeled by fifteen years of autocracy and soured by more than one plot. A young emperor could generally count on a "honeymoon period"; and if we had Agricola's letters from Britain we should get, no doubt, a very different impression of Domitian from that which Tacitus was to give us at the end of the century.

Domitian did, as we know, finally give Agricola three years longer; three years more than either Frontinus or Cerialis. But in his first year or two he had many other things to think of besides that. There was a threat of trouble on the Upper Rhine, for one thing; and Domitian, thirsting for military glory, was not at all sorry. In these circumstances there could be no question of reinforcing Agricola. On the contrary, the Emperor presently informed him that the Army of Britain would have to furnish troops for the Rhine.

Chapter Thirteen

By the Western Sea

EXACTLY how long it took to thresh out the British frontier question and decide on prolonging Agricola's command and giving him permission to go forward, we cannot say; but the summer of consolidation, at the end of which Titus died, was not immediately followed by an advance into Caledonia. It was followed first by a campaign along the west coast, largely sea-borne, and having perhaps for one result the conquest of Galloway. It was only common sense to occupy Galloway, which if left unconquered would be a standing menace to communications with Clydesdale; indeed, it is likely that the conquest had at least been begun in the previous two years. But Agricola now went farther, exploring, it seems, in person some of the great sea-lochs north of the Firth of Clyde, and stationing troops on the coast facing towards Ireland, we are told, with offensive rather than defensive intentions.

But even Agricola, who, as Tacitus says, was one of nature's optimists, can hardly have meditated undertaking campaigns in Ireland and northern Scotland simultaneously. It looks, therefore, as if these were alternative plans; as though, if those authorities at Rome, who thought the Forth-Clyde line too good a frontier not to use, gained the ear of the Emperor, Agricola still hoped for permission to gain new laurels in another direction.

In the mean time, during his fifth summer in Britain, he again made no advance in force beyond the limits of the province as already defined. This is not like him; and when one remembers both the length of time that it must have taken to conduct a high-level argument, and also the fact that this year was the first year of a new emperor, it looks as though he was trying to do something a little better than mark time, while still awaiting a decision on the major issue.

Tacitus' paragraph on the work of this summer is a masterpiece of vagueness, containing as it does no indications of position, except the mention of "the coast opposite Ireland"; but with the help of the evidence supplied by archæologists, it is now possible to make more detailed sense of it. It is instructive also to relate it to the geographical account of north-western Britain given by Ptolemy in the next century.

Here, then, is Tacitus' evidence:

"In his fifth campaign, crossing the sea in the first ship, he subdued tribes hitherto unknown in many successful engagements. He also posted troops on the side of Britain which faces towards Ireland, a measure prompted by hope rather than fear, [of attack from that quarter]. He considered that Ireland, which lies between Britain and Spain and is accessible also by sea from Gaul, would form a connecting-link between these important parts of the empire, with great advantage to each.

"Ireland is a country of smaller area than Britain, but larger than any island of the Mediterranean. Its landscape and climate and the character and culture of its people do not differ greatly from those of Britain. Its sea-approaches and harbours have become comparatively well known through commercial intercourse. Agricola received in friendly fashion an Irish petty king who had been driven out in a civil war, and kept him for use when opportunity offered. I have often heard him say that Ireland could be conquered and held by one legion and a modest force of auxiliary troops; and that it would be advantageous in dealing with Britain too, if Roman forces were on all sides and the spectacle of freedom were, so to say, banished out of sight."

In these words Ireland enters the field of formal European history; and Agricola, it has often been observed, reveals himself as the first of many optimists to have views about it. The references to commerce and to the accessibility of Ireland from France and Spain are of interest, too, as showing that the maritime trade along the Atlantic coast, which goes back to the third millennium before Christ, was still active under the empire. The tombstone of a "merchant in the British trade" at Bordeaux, and a third-century altar set up, also at Bordeaux, to the British goddess Boudig (Success, or Victory), by a merchant of York and Lincoln, show its continuation at a still later date. It was such movements up the west coast of Europe that had, so long ago as the neolithic period, brought the culture of the great-stone-tomb builders to Brittany, Wales, Ireland, western Scotland, and even Caithness and Scandinavia, and which had also brought in that dark "Iberian" element in our western population, which is mentioned more than once in the Irish epics, and which Tacitus attests (no doubt from Agricola himself) as predominating among the Silures of South Wales.

The civilisation of Ireland in the first century was, as Tacitus says, similar to that of Britain; and thanks to the fact that in the event Ireland escaped Roman invasion, we have a picture of at least one side of it from native sources, in the glimpses of daily life embodied in quotations from early laws, and in tales based on the still earlier Ulster epics. The peasantry, largely pre-Celtic, were in subjection, as in Caledonia and in Belgic Britain, to a chariot-driving, largely fair-haired, Celtic aristocracy, descended from the same Central European stock as the men who sacked Rome in the fourth century before Christ and founded Galatia in the third.

Cuchullin, the Hound of Ulster, is described as a little, dark man, and dark too is Naisi, the hero of the Deirdre story; but Cuchullin at least is explicitly described as descended from a family in Alba—Great Britain. The races, fair Celtic-speakers and "dark Iberians", had certainly become much mixed throughout Western Europe before the Roman invasions, and it is likely that many of the Irish peasants already spoke the early Gaelic of their overlords.

The tales give a vivid picture of the barbaric splendours of these Early Iron-Age kings, one of whose favourite sports (as in Homeric Greece) appears to be cattle-raiding, resulting in a warfare which has more than a little in common with the earlier and wilder forms of mediæval tournament. Plain, business-like aggression also occurred, aiming at increasing one's wealth by increasing one's overlordship. Cadet relatives of a conquering king were installed as sub-kings, over the chiefs of a conquered district, or tribute and hostages were exacted from a defeated king who was left in office. In either case, former ruling groups found themselves still in being, but depressed or de-classed, while the peasants had to support two or three strata of land-lords instead of one; and a social pyramid of great height and extreme instability must have risen and fallen more than once in many regions. In these circumstances it is obvious that the expulsion of petty kings by internal sedition must have been no very infrequent occurrence; and Agricola, who, if over-sanguine, was both shrewd and experienced, was not without reasons for believing that in the divided state of the country he could find allies within, and that the Irish kingdoms would go down even more easily than the once imposing realm of Cymbeline.

The days of the Irish High-Kingship in Tara, it should be added, were not yet. There is no trace of it in the Ulster sagas, which are believed to represent the state of things about the beginning of our era. The chronicles which represent it as existing from remote antiquity are believed by good authorities to be based on compilations of the Christian period, after St. Patrick's mission in the fifth century; compilations by genealogists, learned after their fashion, but concerned chiefly to synchronise the genealogies and the king-lists of their country with the great synthesis of classical and Biblical chronology produced by the fourth-century eastern bishop, Eusebius. They are comparable as evidence, that is to say, not to the Irish or Homeric epics, but to Nennius or Geoffrey of Monmouth.

The attempt has naturally and properly been made to identify the disturbance, which provided Agricola with a potentially useful Irish "pretender", with an event mentioned among these legends: the Revolt of the Vassals, in which, according to the story, the entire ruling class of Ireland was invited to a banquet by the rent-paying tribes —one is not surprised to hear that the banquet was two years in preparation—and then treacherously massacred, all except three pregnant women who escaped to Alba. Everything, however, went wrong under the plebeian king (the author carefully tells us): crops failed and there was a general lack of "luck"; and at last the people sent to Alba for a scion of the old royal race to come and rule over them.

In this story, the ostensible dates would fit well enough; and doubtless there were ample grounds for discontent in Ireland; but in other respects it bears all the marks of a fairy-tale. T. F. O'Rahilly, the latest serious scholar to discuss it, dismisses it as such; and Eoin MacNeill, who first put forward the theory, had himself come to mistrust it before the end of his life, regarding the story, at least in the form in which we have it, as a device of the Christian systematisers to account for the fact that the High-Kingship, for which they had been at pains to claim great antiquity, had to start "again" in or about the third century.

It is therefore not possible to synchronise Irish legend with Agricola's campaigns. Ireland was never to become for Agricola more than the goal of his dreams. The dream itself, however, accounts for a marked concentration of early forts on the coast of Cumberland, such as Ellenborough, by Maryport on the River Ellen—probably the Alauna [1] of the Romano-Britons—and Glanoventa (not Clanoventa), now Ravenglass, at the bottom of Eskdale, served by a road over the bleak Wrynose Pass guarded by the fort of Medibogdium (Hardknot). These coastal forts, though not Hardknot, were kept in commission in later centuries for the protection of the western flank of Hadrian's Wall. There was a good deal of piratical raiding from Ireland, developing under the late empire into a serious menace; and Tacitus' statement that Agricola's dispositions were for offensive and not for defensive purposes suggests that there was already some cause for anxiety.

[1] On many maps of Roman Britain, Maryport bears the name Uxellodunum, "High Fort"; but Richmond has recently shown that, in the late Roman document on which this identification is based, a group of names is out of order, and that Uxellodunum is almost certainly Castlesteads on Hadrian's Wall.

Recent discoveries have made it certain, for the first time, that the Romans did indeed occupy Galloway during the same periods, and with the same vicissitudes, as the rest of southern Scotland. Two Roman roads led into south-west Scotland from the land side. One, from their fort at Castledykes, near Lanark, passes another Roman fort at Loudoun Hill, and heads for the coast, but its seaward terminus has not been found. It is most probably under the buildings of the town of Irvine. Its name survives in the form Vindogara or Vindouara in Ptolemy, the name given by him both to Irvine Bay and to a place on or near its shore. The second road forked west from the road up Annandale, crossing the Nith at Carzield (pronounced Careel) five miles above Dumfries, and the Kircudbright-shire Dee at Glenlochar, near Castle Douglas, the only feasible crossing-place for many miles. It was here that air reconnaissance by Dr. J. K. St. Joseph, in 1949, revealed the ground-plan of a Roman fort surrounded by a whole constellation of field entrenchments marking the temporary camps of Roman troops on the move; and that the archæological skill of Professor I. A. Richmond has since shown that the fort existed in the late first and second centuries, being twice destroyed and reconstructed (like many Roman posts in Scotland), and that an Agricolan fort had previously existed close by, on a slightly different site. Dr. St. Joseph has detected one Roman fort still farther west, near Gatehouse of Fleet, and there can be little doubt that more remain to be discovered.

To Glenlochar one would like to attach the name of Carbantoriton, "Wagon Ford", a "town" of the Selgovæ, placed by Ptolemy's *Geography* in just the right position, a little inland from the mouth of the Dee. But it must be added that Ptolemy's indications of latitude and longitude in North Britain are so inaccurate—that is, the information available to him was so lacking in precision—that one cannot claim certainty for this identification.[1]

[1] It has been doubted also on the ground that the smaller tribe of the Novantæ "must" extend east to the River Novius, the Nith. But the root *nov* is far too common among Old Celtic geographical terms for this to be necessary.

As to Agricola's "crossing over on the first ship", that also *might* refer to Galloway. A square earthwork on the hill of Ward Law, at the mouth of the Nith, has been proved to be Roman, and Roman pottery has also come to light at the river-mouth itself, close to Caerlaverock Castle. Edward I, when invading Scotland in 1300, was at particular pains to take Caerlaverock; here again the histories of Roman and mediæval campaigns shed light on one another. It looks as though both Romans and English found it convenient to use the mouth of the Nith as a harbour and landing-place for stores. Sea transport then as now was far cheaper than by land; it could handle heavy stores in bulk; and it could cut out the long detour of the Roman road round the head of the Solway Moss.

There may well have been other ports or "beach-heads" farther west, which have not yet yielded explicit evidence; though casual finds of Roman pottery have been made at several places along the Solway Firth. The Lucopibia of Ptolemy (the name has probably been miscopied), a southern port of the Novantæ, in Wigtownshire, of which the first half means "White", might be a predecessor of Whithorn, where the Romano-Briton St. Ninian later built the little white church that so impressed the Dark Ages. It lay near the south end of the portage—such a portage as prehistoric seafarers were usually glad to make —to Rherigonion, the "Royal Place" of the tribe: a name which survives to this day in those of Stranraer and Loch Ryan.

But the completion of the conquest of South-west Scotland is not likely to have taken all this summer, even if the operations of the two previous years had left anything to finish. Nor would the Novantæ, surely, have been still "an unknown tribe". For part, at least, of this summer's objectives, we must look farther afield. A sentence in the summary account of Britain earlier in Tacitus' *Agricola* runs as follows:

"The character of the outer sea and its tides"—so different from the tideless Mediterranean—"is a subject irrelevant to the present work, and has often been discussed by others. I will add one detail: that nowhere does the sea extend its dominion more widely; it carries the currents of rivers far this way and that; and it does not merely flow up to the shore and ebb back again; it flows in and round, penetrating among the very hills and mountains as though in its own domain."

The phenomena of high tides pouring up a bay or up the estuary of a tidal river could in part be observed in the Bristol Channel or on the Cheshire Sands of Dee, or at Morecambe Bay—the name of which, by the way, is Celtic, meaning "Bend of the Sea" and, as a modern name, was resurrected out of Ptolemy in the eighteenth century. But the detail about the sea flowing in among the mountains, clearly taken from an eye-witness, comes surely from the Firth of Clyde and the great sea-lochs north of it. The Epidii ("Horse-folk") of Kintyre and of a neighbouring island, probably Islay, would be one of the "hitherto unknown tribes"; and even beyond them Ptolemy knows the names of a succession of other tribes on the west coast. He also gives a surprisingly large number of names of the western isles: among others, Maleos (Mull?), Skitis (Skye?), and the Ebudæ or Æbudes ("Hebrides"): another modern resurrected name, the application of which has probably been no more unchanged than the spelling. Ptolemy also has some idea of the picturesque complications of the Firth of Clyde, though he is not able to describe them in full detail. His "Longos Gulf" is not Loch Long, unless by a mistake; it is on the wrong side of Kintyre; but his "Lemannonian Gulf" north of the firth bears a name preserved in that of the river that drains Loch Lomond, the Leven (Gaelic Leamhain) and in Lennox (Leamhnacht), the ancient name of this region.

No tangible traces of Roman encampments have been found on any of these islands or any part of this coast. But somebody had explored the region thoroughly enough for a geographer at Alexandria about A.D. 150 to record genuine names of lochs and islands. It seems likeliest that this was the work of Agricola's fleet. Overnight camps on a beach would not, presumably, reproduce the rectangular lines of the camps of a legion. The coast, too, is often too stony for digging; barricades of rocks and boulders would have to do, and these when deserted would have to suffer storms and erosion as well as the destroying hands of men. Also, many of the best harbours and water-points have been occupied ever since, intensively enough to have obliterated any trace of the passing of Roman sailors. This has happened, for example, at the magnificent castle site of Dumbarton Rock, a miniature Gibraltar, which the Romans must surely have used at all times when they held the Forth–Clyde isthmus.

Thus far speculation. What is *fact* is that Tacitus tells us that Agricola, in the summer when he gazed longingly at Ireland, also personally led sea-borne forces on an expedition in which he "defeated hitherto unknown tribes in many successful battles"; he does not say that they were large battles; and that Ptolemy, about A.D. 150, shows a considerable knowledge of the west coast of Scotland, though it grows progressively sketchier as we get farther north. This is the background of the story which Demetrius told to Plutarch at Delphi in 83, of north-western islands, some of them uninhabited and said to be the abode of spirits; and of how Demetrius himself on an official mission of exploration had visited "the nearest island" (Arran? or Cumbrae?) and found it inhabited by a group of "holy men", unmolested by the tribes of the mainland —forerunners, it seems, of the Christian Celtic hermits of later centuries! While among them, Demetrius saw "signs in the heavens"—perhaps the aurora borealis?—which the hermits assured him were a token that somewhere a great chieftain had passed from this life.

By the end of 82, however, Agricola's correspondence with Domitian had produced a decision, and he was able to turn his attention back from exploration in the west and possibilities in Ireland to the (no doubt long projected) invasion of Caledonia.

Domitian was adamant about demanding a considerable legionary draft from the Army of Britain for the campaign of 83. He, in person, would be crossing the Upper Rhine early that summer. But by way of compensation, he gave Agricola leave to raise additional British levies and to employ them in Britain. This had been contrary to army practice of late, since the rebellion on the Rhine, when local auxiliaries had made common cause with the free Germans. Agricola, however, was confident in his Britons, or at least in some of the traditionally friendly tribes; and he did successfully use South British troops in Scotland—a notable testimony to the success of the constructive side of his work as governor.

Further, Domitian would be sending him some newly conscripted—indeed, newly conquered—German levies, who were *not* considered reliable; hence the decision to send them oversea, where, if they deserted, they could not walk home. What Agricola thought of this accession to his paper strength, we are not told, and he was probably not asked; but we know what he did with them. He used them to garrison back areas, thus releasing better troops for the front.

This, then, was how a new and very raw cohort from the Rhineland tribe of the Usipi came to be occupying, within the year 83, one of Agricola's new forts by the Irish Sea. The result was an exciting and horrible episode, which caught the imagination of the Roman reading public sufficiently to be recorded not only by Tacitus but, long after, by Dio. It happened in 83, while the governor was in eastern Scotland; but as it forms a pendant to his Irish Sea operations, it may be recounted here.

Many Roman centurions, as the world is aware, had many fine qualities. Not a few, at the same time, were quite capable of provoking their troops to murder, as happened in the great mutiny in the Rhine army in the days of Tiberius. Discipline was brutal; even in the legions corporal punishment could be administered, at his own sole discretion, by the centurion of each company, with the vinestick which was the official symbol of his rank. It may be imagined, then, what things were like during the process of "licking into shape" a new battalion of men who were still in many ways less like trained soldiers than like prisoners of war.

The question has often been asked, how this prisoner-of-war battalion managed to be already in north-west Britain before the fall of 83, when Domitian's operations on the Rhine had not begun till the spring. A possible answer is that there may have been preliminary operations to prepare the way for the Emperor, which, because they were carried out before his personal arrival, have left no mark in history. It will be seen, however, that the presence of this unit makes it likelier that Agricola's Sixth Campaign was in 83, and therewith, that he arrived in Britain in 78 and not in 77 (cf. p. 87).

So, at a new square fort, by a harbour somewhere on the coast of Galloway or Cumberland, something over four hundred Germans suffered the discipline administered by bad n.c.o.s (not the best n.c.o.s; they would be at the front) of a very tough army, and longed for their homes— nice, messy, round huts of some hamlet in a forest glade. In charge of them was a batch of old soldiers, holding all the posts in the hierarchy, as extra-pay man, double-pay man, watch-corporal, standard-bearer, up to deputy-centurion. At the head of all was another centurion, in acting command. The post was evidently considered beneath the dignity of a Roman Knight.

No doubt these n.c.o.s all knew that the Germans hated them; but marooned in an island, they never expected them to dare to start anything. Perhaps the critical period of desperation might have passed if, one day when things were bad, three galleys of the Irish Sea fleet had not put into the harbour. It was now or never. The Germans rose, with a concerted and efficient fury of which their tormentors had not believed them capable, killed all Romans on the station, and seized all three ships, with their helmsmen—alive. This was important, since the helmsmen were also the navigators. Then they all went on board and set off to make their way back to Germany by rowing round Scotland.

The voyage, as one might expect with such crews, was a long-drawn tale of hardship and disaster. They naturally did not trust their pressed helmsmen, and before long had killed two of them on suspicion of attempted treachery. The third survived by desperate obedience. Language difficulties prevented their presenting themselves as allies to the Britons; and when they needed more food, they had to take it by force—if they could. Resistance was fierce and surprise difficult to effect. Often they were repulsed, and went hungry. Presently, in desperation, they resorted to cannibalism, starting on those of their comrades who looked likely to die anyhow, later drawing lots. But the weather at least seems to have been kind; for they actually did succeed in rounding Cape Wrath and making their way across the North Sea to the Frisian coast.

Here final disaster overtook them. Those shoal waters were more treacherous to unskilled crews than the ferocious-looking coast of Scotland, where shelter could often be found in the sea-lochs. All the ships were wrecked, and though most of the men seem to have got ashore, it was only to be seized as slaves and potential merchandise by the Frisians and other Low-German tribes, to whom Rhinelanders were merely foreigners. And so in the normal course of trade "some of them", says Tacitus, "passed on from one buyer to another, reached our side of the Rhine; and so became known the details of their remarkable adventure". But whether the unfortunate men were then executed, as one might expect, for mutiny and murder, he does not deign to say.

Chapter Fourteen

The Invasion of Caledonia

IT was a pity to have to surrender so many legionaries for the Rhine, but Agricola knew that it was no use arguing; especially with a young emperor and one liable to take umbrage. He set himself to plan the campaign on the basis of a striking force of three legions, all three perhaps somewhat under strength, and one certainly very much so. This would enable him to leave the main body of one legion in the south, in case of any stirrings of trouble in Wales or Northumbria.

He had numerous auxiliary regiments; in Hadrian's time, the army in this big, thinly-populated province contained more than twice as many auxiliaries as legionaries; but many of them would have to be used on lines of communication in the recently conquered territories. For the crowning battle in the following year, he was able to concentrate probably the same three legions, less detachments sent to Germany and guards left at their depôts—perhaps 8,000 to 10,000 men in all—plus 8,000 light infantry and as many as 5,000 cavalry.

Using every available weapon to compensate for his deficiency in legionaries, Agricola also brought up his fleet on the east coast. The fleet had naturally been important in Roman Britain, since the earliest days, but only as a transport service. Agricola, Tacitus tells us, was the first to "make it part of his forces"; in modern terms, to give it an operational rôle. Using the experience gained in western waters, he would employ it not only for transport but for raiding, keeping the natives guessing, as unopposed sea-power so well can, where the next blow would fall.

As to strategy, Agricola was in no doubt. Reconnaissance and interrogation of natives, for which there had been

plenty of time in the two last summers, had left the
Romans with no illusions about the tangle of mountains
and glens, roadless, all but trackless, the valleys choked
with bog and birch thickets, that lay behind the Highland
Line. Roman forts were not outposts in the tactical sense,
it has to be remembered. They were battalion posts, meant
to afford a secure base for patrolling or for offensive or
counter-offensive operations. Reconnaissance over the
northern territories of the Damnonii must often have
brought Roman patrols to such places as the Pass of Leny
or the hill-foot by Aberfoyle, where Highlands and Lowlands meet at a line almost as clear as the desert and the
sown along the Nile Valley.

No conquering army has ever marched through the
Perthshire Highlands; the Pass of Killiecrankie was the
grave of one army which tried. General Wade penetrated
them with one of his famous roads only in time of peace.
Half-tamed, they are pretty enough country for hill-
walkers; wholly wild, they were no sort of place to take
long columns of men and animals. But to the east,
broad valleys run roughly parallel to the east coast, skirting
the north-eastern prolongation of the Highland Line, and
running between a broken range of lower hills of volcanic
rock—the Ochils and the Sidlaws—and the great meta-
morphic mass of the Highlands themselves. By this way
have come English armies on their rare excursions north
of the Forth, from Edward I, who once marched as far as
Elgin, to the Duke of Cumberland.

Armies, railways, Roman roads and prehistoric trade-
routes show, in mountain country, a strong tendency to
follow the same general lines, laid down for them by the
local geology; and so it is here. Half the famous battle-
names in Scottish history lie along or not far from Agricola's line of advance: Kilsyth, Falkirk, Bannockburn,
Stirling Bridge, Sheriffmuir, Tippermuir, Nechtansmere,
Methven; farther north, Harlaw, Inverurie, Alford, Fyvie,
Auldearn. Culloden is probably farther than the Romans
penetrated. Clear traces of a Roman road and a line of
Agricolan forts mark his route as far as the great legionary
station of Inchtuthil, where the Tay leaves the Highlands,

and a newly discovered cohort-post twelve miles farther
north-east at Cardean. Farther than this there are only
marching-camps; i.e. no Roman occupation was ever consolidated. The known camps, their numbers increased by
Dr. St. Joseph's air-photography, continue at regular,
roughly twelve-mile intervals as though all formed a single
series, perhaps re-used, almost to the Moray Firth, ending
with doubtful traces at Fochabers by Elgin.

Agricola's strategy, as we can now see from the tangible
relics of his passage, was to advance by this eastern route,
blocking as he went, with a fort, every valley-entrance to
the Highlands on his left by which the light-footed Caledonians might try to reach his lines of communication.
Meanwhile his fleet would raid and threaten points on the
coast, discouraging the coastal peoples from concentrating
against him. Thus he would penetrate finally to Aberdeenshire, the old province of Buchan, the heart and granary
of the north-east, just as it still was that of the Pictish kingdom in the Dark Ages. The mountain country, though it
might be impracticable to penetrate it, could then be
blockaded. A few irreconcilables might hold out in the
glens, but many could not; they must submit or starve.

It may be asked how a fort, without firearms, could block
a pass. Surely, it may be argued, enemies in small numbers
could slip past by night, and enemies in large numbers
could demonstrate against the fort while others passed?

This is perfectly true. Forts without firearms—or even
with them—do not entirely stop infiltration. What they, or
rather their garrisons, can do is to make it slow, difficult
and dangerous, and especially to inflict losses on raiders
who, when counter-attacked by mobile forces, are trying
to get back. There would be a great deal of difference, for
example, between bolting into the woods below the Pass
of Leny, and trying to reach the Pass of Leny, pursued by
Roman cavalry, past a wide patch of cleared woodland
round the fort of Bochastle, manned by some four hundred resolute men including some archers and possessing
a few "scorpions"—the Roman man-killing catapult. Small
parties would be liable to be intercepted by the garrisons
of the forts; and large forces, with their best lines of re-

treat blocked by the forts themselves, might be forced to crowd at defiles and be most disastrously caught.

Full of hope, in the spring of 83 Agricola sent out his orders. The forts on the isthmus were evacuated (excavation has shown that their Agricolan occupation was very brief); and their garrisons joined the field army, initially of perhaps 30,000 men, which concentrated in the neighbourhood of Falkirk. The IXth Legion from York sent off its detachment for the Rhine, under a young tribune, L. Roscius Aelianus, while its main body joined the concentration. Legionary detachments were usually of 1,000 or 2,000; and detachments of 2,000 each from two of the British legions and perhaps 1,000 each from the other two would make up a force large enough for an Emperor to trouble about. Allowing for sick, for vacancies on the establishment and for a guard at the depôt, there may not have been many more than 2,000 men of the IXth left to follow its Eagle. For his other two legions Agricola presumably had his old corps, the XXth, and II, Adiutrix, from Chester; II, Augusta, no doubt depleted at least as much as IX, would be the natural choice to leave in the south.

With this force, Agricola, "in the summer which saw the beginning of his sixth year in command, took in the tribes beyond the Forth; and because a general movement of the northern tribes and a march to meet him was to be feared, he reconnoitred the harbours with his fleet". First of these, naturally, would be the Firth of Tay, which river is navigable and tidal as far as Perth.

By land the main axis of advance, between the hills and the Firth of Forth, ran over undulating and lightly wooded country to the historic crossing of the river below Stirling Castle. The Romans undoubtedly used that splendid acropolis, though later occupation has left no trace of their presence. Their road from the south runs purposefully straight for the castle rock; moreover, the rock itself is not only a natural fortress but a magnificent natural signalling-station; and the Roman army was very signal-conscious. A signal-tower on the rise south of the Bannock Burn had the function of transmitting messages between Stirling and Camelon, the next fort to the south; and farther north, in

Strath Earn, a whole series of such posts testifies to the particular sensitiveness of the Romans about their communications in this region.

Stirling, no doubt, had been occupied in advance, and the Forth bridged; no great matter to an army that could bridge the Danube. The advance proceeded, west of the Ochil Hills, up Allan Water to a camp at Ardoch—probably another Alauna, named from its river. A cohort was left there to dig itself in, in a permanent fort whose defences (further strengthened by later Romans) are the best preserved among all Roman forts in Scotland. Heading now north-east, the army reached the Earn at Strageath, and turned down-stream. Temporary forts at Strageath and Gask and the earth foundations and post-holes of many signal towers show, as above-mentioned, particular care over communications with Ardoch and Stirling. Then they bore north-east again over another undulation, and cheered, one fancies, to see from the high ground the ships of their fleet already in the Tay.

Meanwhile Agricola, after his custom—for he took a pride in personally siting his forts—will have been out with the covering forces on that left flank which might at any moment become the front. Forts were planted in the jaws of the valleys at Bochastle, by Callander; at Dalginross in Glen Artney, overlooking the Earn; and at Fendoch, where Glenalmond narrows to the gorge of the "Sma' Glen", a postern gate of the Highlands through which General Wade ran one of his famous roads. Of these, the traces of the forts at Bochastle and Fendoch, though long rumoured to exist, have only lately been proved by archæology. Bochastle has been almost obliterated by floods; but Fendoch, carefully excavated by Richmond, is the one and only Agricolan fort, not overlaid by later works, of which we have hitherto a complete plan.

Yet another fort would be "in order", between Callander and Loch Lomond—perhaps near Aberfoyle; but of such an one no sign has yet been found.

Some time fairly early in this campaign too—but it can hardly have been before June—there was personal news of major importance for Agricola. He had left his wife once more expecting a baby. The news was of its birth. After twenty-one years of married life, Agricola and Domitia had again a son.

Tacitus records a memory of this confident spring. "It was a glorious sight, when the advance went forward both by land and sea; and often in the same camp, horse, foot and marines would mingle and make merry together, boasting, each of their own achievements and adventures; capping each other's stories of forest and mountain fastnesses or of storms at sea; of victory over the enemy or of conquest of the Ocean, in the regular manner of soldiers' tales."

"The Britons, too," he adds, "as was learned from prisoners, were dismayed by the appearance of the fleet, feeling that now the secrets of their seas were laid open, and their last retreat cut off. The peoples of Caledonia resorted to arms on a grand scale, still further exaggerated by reports, as usual with the unknown. They even took the offensive, attacking a Roman fort, which had some effect on our morale; and the faint-hearted urged, on the plea of prudence, that it would be wise to retire behind the Forth in our own time, rather than be driven."

The post thus attacked, as it appears, fiercely and in considerable strength, was presumably one of the barrier-forts in the entrances to the glens. Had it fallen, it would have let the enemy through on to Agricola's lines of communication; and the seriousness of this is shown by words later put into Agricola's mouth by Tacitus, referring to the difficulties of supply on his northward venture, and adding: "It is a well-tried principle of mine that a general's or an army's rear is never safe."

The peoples of Caledonia, then, had a social system capable of concerting large-scale resistance, of raising an army fit to face Agricola's, and (which is really the most remarkable) of supporting it in the field for considerable periods. They had also leaders capable of framing and carrying out a coherent and sensible strategy. Tacitus names one of them in the following year—Calgacus ("Swordsman"), a fighting king of ancient lineage. These chiefs did not rush headlong upon the armoured ranks of the Romans. They made repeated efforts to find a point where they could break through Agricola's cordon and get at his rear; and the threat shook the nerve of some of Agricola's legion commanders, just as similar threats invariably shook the nerve of Italian officers in Abyssinia during World War II. It was only when fairly brought to bay by Agricola's cautious, methodical advance, that they at last manned a hill-position and prepared to fight it out.

Who were these Caledonians?

Those whom the Romans chiefly noticed, that is the chiefs and most of their fighting-men, were, it is clear from Tacitus, the same tall, fair, Germanic-looking Celts, whom Agricola had encountered throughout eastern Britain and whom we hear of even in Ireland. "The reddish hair and large limbs of the people of Caledonia bespeak", he says, "a German origin." The few names of Caledonians that we hear from Roman sources are Celtic too: e.g. Calgacus bears a name known also in Ireland, "Calgaich". (The form Galgacus is a scribe's mistake.) But Dio, when describing the Emperor Severus' march over the same ground, mentions also a very primitive element in the population; hunters and food-gatherers, practising no agriculture, nomadic, "naked and barefoot", and probably using "classificatory" kinship-terms. Dio, who had not been here himself, fails to distinguish between these savages and the "higher barbarian" culture of the chariot-driving chieftains; but being an important official in Rome at the time, he probably had some genuine information. It was perhaps from some fusion of Celts and earlier natives that the rulers of the later "Pictish" kingdom in eastern Scotland emerged, with their custom (*not* unparalleled among early Celts and Germans) of tracing descent through the mother.

What language these later Picts spoke is a question with which we are not obliged to deal here. All we know (from Bede) is that it was different both from the Gaelic of the Scots, immigrant from Ireland before Bede's time, and from the Old British, ancestral to Welsh, which place-names show to have been spoken in Scotland as well as

England in the Roman period. Pictish may still have been a Celtic language. But it is perhaps worth while to point out that nothing but unnecessary mystification, and a great deal of that, has resulted from attempts to treat the word "Picts" as a term of scientific ethnology for "pre-Celtic Britons". "Picts", the Latin word meaning "painted men", first appears as a term denoting North Britons in a writer of the third century. It looks as if it had started simply as a slang term, current among "Romans" (i.e. Romanised Britons) for their despised but dreaded cousins beyond the Forth. It covers *all* native Britons outside the Roman sphere of influence, irrespective of their language or culture. One of the chief tribes of the Picts, located in the central Highlands, is called the Dicalydones, which reminds one of the "Duecaledonian Ocean", Ptolemy's name for the sea beyond Scotland. Both words seem to embody the name of the Caledonii or Caledones (both forms were in use) with a prefix indicating that they were divided into two chief cantons; and for this great tribe, whose territory extended, according to Ptolemy, from Lennox to Moray, to be so divided is by no means surprising.

Now, the name "Britons" (which also appears in many forms: Pretanoi, Brittones, Britanni, Welsh Prydein, Gaelic Cruithne, etc.) also appears to have meant "painted men". It was current already among the continental Celts in the days of the great explorer Pytheas, as a name for the more barbarous peoples of these islands. But it certainly was used and accepted by the Celts who settled in Britain. When, therefore, the later Christian Picts traced their descent from a mythical "King Cruithne", this merely means that the Picts' own name for themselves was "Britons". It is not scientific to equate either the general term Cruithne or, still more, the abusive Latin term Picts, always and everywhere, with "pre-Celtic peoples".

It was no small coalition that now faced Agricola. Tacitus rightly calls them "the peoples of Caledonia", meaning all Scotland north of the Forth, not "Caledonii"; though the name of this great Highland tribe was well known in his time—known, for instance, to the poet Martial. Important among them must have been the lowland Vacomagi in Angus and the Mearns, whose land Agricola entered when he crossed the Tay, and the Tæxali of Buchan, as far as Kinnaird Head. Irreconcilable exiles from the conquered south there will have been, too, and perhaps even adventurers from the farther tribes; the Decantæ of Ross, the Lugi of Sutherland, and the inland Smertæ, who used to smear their faces with the blood of the slain. The tall, fair or red-haired chiefs in primitive tartan, their shields and helmets gay with enamel, drove their pairs of small, tough, fast-moving ponies; they were followed by thousands of half-naked, barefoot infantry, bearing small, square, wooden shields, with a metal boss over the hand-grip, and spears, with a knob at the butt end, which could be clashed with terrifying noise.

Having failed to rush one of Agricola's barrier forts, Calgaich and his colleagues called off their men. If they could not break through by surprise, they certainly could not do so without it. They waited their opportunity when Agricola should reach more open country; there, moving in several columns, they hoped that some at least of them could get through to his rear.

Unfortunately for them, though they could plan a sensible strategy, it was beyond the powers of a barbarian high command to keep it a secret. Agricola very soon heard of it, no doubt from the interrogation of prisoners. "Meanwhile"—that is, apparently at the very staff-conference at which some officers counselled retreat—"he received information that the enemy proposed to break through in several bodies. Accordingly, lest his flanks should be turned by the enemy's superior numbers and knowledge of the country, he also divided his army into three columns, and so advanced."

In face of this movement to sweep the country on a wide front, the Caledonian chiefs were not slow to think again. By reconnaissance they soon noticed that one of the Roman columns—that of which the nucleus was formed by the depleted IXth Legion—was distinctly smaller than the others. "By a swift change of plan, under cover of night they united their forces and fell with their whole strength upon the IXth Legion, as being the weakest. Before the troops were fairly awake they had killed the sentries, burst into the startled camp, and were fighting actually within the lines. But Agricola, informed by his scouts that the enemy had moved, was following on their track."

The reconnaissance and intelligence work of both sides during these operations seems to have been of a high order, but the Britons had again failed to reckon with that of their enemy. One wonders if they made any attempt to deceive Agricola by leaving a skeleton force facing him. If so, it was unsuccessful. Agricola, who never in his recorded life shows up better than on this night, divined at once what they had gone to do; he had probably been worried about the IXth all along; and without hesitation he launched his own legion and attached troops upon the hazards of a night march.

In the camp of the IXth men woke to shouting and the clash of arms, and grabbed helmet, shield and sword. There would be no time for buckling on body-armour before the pickets were overwhelmed and the enemy were among the tents. One imagines the raucous bellow of the centurions, never so welcome, with a "To me! To me!" rallying the companies until, much impeded by tents and guy-ropes, they formed as solid a schiltron as might be, presenting the shield-wall that was the Roman soldiers' best defence. So they fought for their lives against half-seen enemies who sprang upon isolated men and leapt in between the rallying groups, that grew in size as more men made their way to the standards and the centurions' shout.

Meanwhile Agricola and his division—perhaps seven or eight thousand horse and foot—made their best speed across trackless country, the centurions doing their best to keep the men closed up; a nightmare business for so large a force by night among thickets and boggy patches and intermittent streams. The camps may not have been more than a few miles apart, but the darkness of the short summer night was turning grey before they came within earshot of the battle.

"The moon shone clear, the day drew near,
    The spears in flinders flew."
—and Agricola, feeling that minutes might be important,

ordered his cavalry and the swiftest light infantry to go ahead. Then he called upon the legion for a concerted cheer. In the camp, among the fighters, those not too immediately engaged to do so turned their heads. It was almost sunrise; and far off, Agricola's standards could be seen, riding high above the torrent of men. The moral effect was tremendous. "The Britons were dismayed by the threat to their rear; the IXth took heart and, no longer in fear of their lives, fought for their honour. They went over to the offensive, and there was furious fighting in the confined space of the camp gateways, until the enemy broke before the united efforts of both forces, fighting in rivalry, the one for the credit of effecting a rescue and the other to prove that they had not required it. It was a victory which would have finished the war had not marshes and forests covered the enemy's retreat."

The last sentence is not one of Tacitus' most helpful; it amounts to saying that if things had been quite different they would have been quite different. But his next paragraph, on the moral effects of this battle, is of more interest:

"The realisation or the report of this achievement raised the spirit of the army to such a pitch that they felt nothing was impossible to them. They clamoured for a march right through Caledonia till they discovered the utmost end of Britain, in one continuous series of battles. The prudent wiseacres of yesterday were loud and eager after the event. This is one of the major injustices of a soldier's life: everybody claims a share in successes, while reverses are attributed to one alone. The Britons, however, felt that their defeat was in no wise due to the Romans being the better men, but to the fortune of war and the skill of Agricola, and were not in the least dispirited. They continued to arm their young men, to remove their women and children to places of safety, and at meetings for religious rites to solemnise the league and covenant of the tribes. So the campaign ended with both sides in fighting mood."

The scene of this battle is uncertain; but it may well have been still south-west of the Tay. There was a Roman station called Victoria somewhere in the north-east corner of the Damnonian country, which cannot have extended much beyond Strath Earn. If this commemorated Agricola's victory in A.D. 83, then the sweeping movement which he was carrying out was designed to clear the triangle of country between the Tay, the Earn and the Highland Line; the fort called "Fort Victory" will have been at Strageath; and the numerous signal-stations along Strathearn will have been designed with special reference to these operations.

Beyond the Tay, the advance continued north-east up the "Great Valley", Strathmore. Strathmore itself was probably occupied in that year; but that was all. The fierce counter-offensive of the Caledonians, and the repeated redeployments which it had forced upon the Romans, had at least been highly successful in using up time.

Agricola left a legion, as well as auxiliaries, to winter in the north and hold the ground now; probably the veteran XXth, while the IInd and IXth returned to their bases.

The new fortress was at Inchtuthil on the Tay, a site proved as Agricolan in 1952 by Richmond and St. Joseph. It had an easy supply-line to Carpow, on the Firth, whose post-Roman name means the Fort at the Pool; its Roman name may have been Horrea, "The Granaries". Inchtuthil itself is probably the "Winged Camp" of later geographers, the "wings" being a technical term for merlons. It formed a major bastion of the fortress-barrier along the Highland Line, facing the point where Glengarry and the Pass of Killiecrankie afforded a route for highlanders, if not for invaders, from rather than to the north.

The summer's work did not give course for unqualified satisfaction. A victory had been won, but a disaster had been narrowly averted; and the natives had displayed not only gallantry but a political cohesion and strategic skill which were disconcerting. In spite of valuable support from the fleet, the resources of the weakened invasion-army had been taxed to the full; and the ground gained and consolidated still did not extend far beyond the Tay.

Still, Inchtuthil and Carpow could be good bases for a further advance; and the explorations of the fleet had shown that the Moray Firth, beyond the main mass of the Highlands, was only eighty miles away.

With mixed feelings, Agricola rode south for the winter to his civilian duties, and his wife and the son he had not yet seen.

Chapter Fifteen

Climax

THERE was all the usual business to occupy the winter. Among other things, there was a new Law Officer to meet—L. Iavolenus Priscus, later a legal authority of some fame, many of whose decisions are quoted in the law-books. He also increased his renown by severely shocking the younger Pliny by making a joke while an author was giving a reading of his poems. He had just been transferred to Britain from command of the troops in Africa, and since he would be the acting-governor of South Britain during the next campaign, there would naturally be much to talk over.

Then there were the new British regiments, from the friendly tribes, to inspect; Agricola thought well of them, and decided that in the next summer they could be put in the line of battle. He could not expect many more years in Britain; if he was to effect his ambition and win lasting fame by completing the conquest, he badly needed a victory in the coming year; and with a tough and resourceful enemy and an ever lengthening line of communication, he was going to need every available man.

To these professional anxieties, private trouble was added as the spring advanced. The baby, the new son, was ailing; and while Agricola was about to start for the north, it died. It was a cruel blow to the parents, and Agricola made no attempt to disguise it. The dogma of the extreme Stoics, that the wise man, conformed to the will of God, is impervious to sorrow, was not one which he could share; and he disdained to pose. But he did not let himself be crushed, and in the new campaign he found the best anodyne. One feels the more sorry for Domitia, left alone again amid the empty pomp of the governor's residence.

Sending his fleet ahead, as in the previous year, to harry

the coast and keep the enemy guessing, Agricola advanced
from the Tay with a mobile army, including the British
regiments. Tacitus says nothing about the events of the
early summer; evidently they did not make an exciting
story. Later there is a hint of weeks of marching, in a
speech put into the mouth of Agricola. "Many a time on
the march, as you toiled over the hills and through bogs
and rivers. I have heard brave men say, 'When will the
enemy be delivered into our hands?' Well, here they
come!" There is a hint, too, of a long and precarious line
of communications. We may surmise that the Caledonians
showed all their old skill in sudden attacks on the flank
and threats to the rear of the invaders; for what Tacitus
does reveal later is that the reason was far advanced by the
time Agricola at last achieved his object. It must have been
far north of Inchtuthil that he brought the enemy to
battle, presumably by threatening some objective which
they could not abandon, such as the standing corn in the
fields of Aberdeenshire; for they were not so foolish as to
engage in the fearful carnage of a pitched battle against
the armoured Romans so long as the Romans could be
kept out of their country by any other means.

As a last resort, then, the Caledonians and their allies
took up a hill position and prepared to fight it out. The
place was called the Graupian or, more correctly, the
Craupian Hill. From a hint in the imaginary speech given
by Tacitus to Calgacus, it seems to have been fairly near
the sea; but its position remains uncertain, although we
owe to its name a term firmly established on our maps: the
name "Grampian", which, like "Hebrides", was originally
a misapplication of a mis-spelling. We are not compelled
even to look for a position which blocked Agricola's
route; it may quite well have flanked it. Agricola, as we
have seen, was sensitive about his rear, and if an enemy
army did take up a position flanking his line of march, it
would be essential for him to deal with it before proceeding. In any case, the Caledonians were surely aware that a
pitched battle was what their enemy wanted.

So Agricola "reached the Craupian Hill, which the
enemy had already occupied. For the Britons, undismayed

by the result of the previous battle, and expecting only death or slavery, had learned that they must make common cause in face of the common danger. By the sending of embassies and the conclusion of treaties they had called out the united forces of all their states. Already more than 30,000 armed men were to be seen, and still they were flowing in—all the young men, all whose old age was yet green and vigorous; famous warriors, proudly wearing the spoils of their valour—when one of their leaders, Calgacus, a chieftain of proud descent and outstanding prowess, is reported to have addressed the assembled multitude, clamorous for battle, after this fashion. . . ."

What follows is a fine tirade against Roman imperialism, but it is imaginary: an example of the bad habit of ancient historians of casting general reflections on issues at stake into the form of fictitious speeches. Agricola, whose speech duly follows, even answers points made by Calgaich, as if he had heard him. But it remains a fine tirade, and is of interest for its Tacitean summary of the grievances of the Britons: the conscription; tribute in money and in corn; Roman offences against women; slavery in the mines, or the corvée, driving roads through the forests and draining swamps under the lash of the whip and of the task-master's tongue. The very slaves of the Romans would bait a new slave. (There had been considerable Roman activity in draining the Fens in eastern England, as Tacitus probably knew, but it seems hardly likely that Calgaich did.) There is also a famous sentence, which may contain a reference to the clearing of areas along military frontiers: "For robbery, massacre and rapine they abuse the name of empire; and where they have made a desert they call it peace."

The British position was on hills, clear of wood or scrub, rising, fairly steeply in places, from level ground. Their array rose tier above tier; "an imposing and also a daunting spectacle," says our historian, "while the level ground in the midst was full of the noise and disorderly movement of chariotry". The vague expression "in the midst" appears to mean "in the British centre". It does not mean "between the two armies"; for the first fighting, we find, was between infantry on both sides, while the chariots were not engaged till a little later. Later again we read of Britons "on the tops of the hills", not engaged at first, but descending later to threaten the Roman flanks, and thus exposing themselves to the charge of cavalry. It seems therefore that the British line must have been defending a col or pass, in undulating rather than mountainous country, with their chariots (the aristocratic arm) in the centre, infantry on the hills, "tier above tier", and a further screen of infantry extending across the whole front at the foot of the slope.

Towards this position the Roman army moved up in ponderous array, the heavily equipped legions covered by cavalry and light infantry; halted just out of arrow-range from the hills; and dug in. It was probably not till after a night's rest that Agricola marshalled them in line of battle. He had enough troops, but only just enough, to be able to draw up his own army, like the enemy's, in depth, in two lines of not very unequal strength. Eight thousand light infantry—a far larger number must have been left holding forts—formed the first line, flanked by 1,500 cavalry on each wing. Not to be dangerously outflanked, he had to make it rather a thin line, and most of his senior officers were for bringing up the legions at once; but Agricola, naturally optimistic, as Tacitus says—and confident also in his veteran soldiers—stuck to his decision to let his relatively cheap and expendable "native troops" take the first shock. The fact that, not to be dangerously outflanked, the line had to be made thin, gives us some idea, if rather a vague one, of the front to be covered; on the basis of four infantrymen or two troopers per yard, which would be a thin line by ancient standards, the front would be something like two miles in length, and any attempt to identify the battlefield must take into account this fact. Farther back, just in front of the entrenchments, the eagles of three legions gleamed and towered among the other standards, above the ranks of some 8,000 or 10,000 armoured men; and four more cavalry "wings"—another 1,000 lances on each flank—were held in reserve against an emergency which Agricola accurately foresaw.

Agricola's estimate that the enemy numbered over

30,000 sounds like a heavy exaggeration; the total fighting strength of the highland clans in the eighteenth century was estimated, in a report submitted to the government, at no more than that. But he was facing a coalition of the tribes, the eastern Tæxali and Vacomagi (if they were not by now subdued) as well as Caledonians and perhaps men of the northern tribes; the levies that manned the hills represented a notable war effort. Agricola took his position seriously enough to warn his troops (assuming that we may take his alleged speech more seriously than his opponent's) that a defeat here, in unexplored country, where there were already difficulties of supply, would be disastrous. They must win, for their life's sake as well as for their honour—and if not, then "it will not be inglorious to fall here, at the very limits of the world". With that he sent away his horse, so that the men might see that he was keeping no private means of escape (Cæsar had done the same in more than one of his battles) and took up his position on foot in front of the standards; that is, between the legions in rear and the auxiliary regiments in his front line.

"As the armies came together," continues Tacitus, "the action began with a discharge of missiles. The Britons stood their ground, skilfully dodging our javelins or parrying them with their long swords and small targes, and replied with a storm of weapons, until Agricola called upon four Batavian and two Tungrian (Belgian) battalions to close with the enemy; thus the advantage would lie with his veteran troops, for the British swords, having no point [long swords for slashing, in the old Celtic manner] were unhandy at close quarters." The Batavian cohorts, from the Rhine delta, were considered among the toughest in the Roman army. Three of them disappear from Britain later, perhaps withdrawn for the Danubian wars; one, along with the two Tungrian units, from Tongres in the Ardennes, remained for centuries, marrying locally and worshipping strange gods, ranging from German Valkyries to the Persian Mithras, at their forts on Hadrian's Wall.

Agricola thus "leads" in the centre, his object being, initially, to draw all the enemy's troops into action before committing his own second line.

The Batavi charged with deadly effect: "mixing the fighting, jabbing with the spikes of their shields, stabbing at the enemy's faces. They overwhelmed the Britons on the level, and began to fight their way uphill. The other cohorts, fired by their example, smote down the enemy opposite to them; and some of these were left not dead, some even unwounded, by the speed of the advance. Meanwhile the cavalry . . ."

Unfortunately, just what the cavalry did is kept from us. The next word in the book as we have it is "fled", with no reason given as to why they should have. Many suggestions have been made; but it seems at least to the present writer that a whole line or more has been omitted in copying. It probably had some reference to skirmishing, in contrast to the stationary position which follows. Tacitus continues: "The chariotry now joined in the infantry battle; and though their first advance [i.e. that of the Romans?] had been terrifying, they were brought to a standstill by the dense masses of the enemy and the unfavourable ground. The scene was now by no means like that of a cavalry action. The men, already advancing with difficulty or halted, were borne down by the bodies of the horses; and often runaway chariots or riderless horses would plunge into them, impelled by terror, from front or flank."

The phrase "by no means like a cavalry battle", is curious; so much so that many editors have suspected an error and tried to correct the text. But this is needless. The fact is simply that Tacitus, like most Roman and late Greek writers, had been brought up in the idea that a good style is a style liberally interlarded with clichés from the classical authors; and this phrase, which is used by (literally) all the best stylists among Roman historians, is a famous cliché from a famous personal narrative of the campaigns of Alexander the Great. It is invariably used of mounted troops brought to a standstill in battle and no longer able to manœuvre.

"The Britons, also, who had not yet been engaged but had remained above on the hills, gazing contemptuously at the small numbers of the Romans, now began to descend and work round the flanks of the advancing troops; but

Agricola had expected exactly this move, and threw in against them four regiments of cavalry, which he had held in reserve for emergencies. Their charge scattered the Britons in a flight as swift as their advance had been impetuous; and the plan of the Britons was now turned against them, for the cavalry, by his orders, went on from the battle-front and attacked the enemy in rear."

This manœuvre, that of taking the outflankers themselves in flank with troops held back for the purpose, and the principle, that of drawing the last of the enemy into action while still one's self keeping something in hand, were both already classic. Alexander, Hannibal, Cæsar had all won victories by similar tactics; and Agricola had naturally read about them in the standard books.

Before the terror and surprise of this new assault, the whole British line gave way. Outflanked as they were, many were cut off; some Romans, having taken prisoners (a saleable commodity), were constrained to kill them on encountering others. Some in a berserk fury hurled themselves on the Romans with their bare hands and were cut down; most made for the woods in rear of their position, keeping together in masses, and still dangerous. At the edge of the forest they rallied, and ambushed the first rash leaders of the pursuit; and the Romans "might have suffered considerable loss through over-confidence. But Agricola was everywhere. He sent in his light infantry in force, like cordons of beaters. Where the forest was dense, he dismounted some of his cavalry; where it was more open, he bade his horsemen sweep it. But when the Britons saw the pursuit developing again in ordered lines, they fled, not in formed bodies as before, nor waiting for each other. Scattered and avoiding one another, they made for the remotest wilds. Only nightfall and weariness put an end to the pursuit.

"Enemy losses were of the order of 10,000 killed; on our side, 360 fell, including Aulus Atticus, the commander of a cohort, who was carried by his youthful bravery and by his spirited charger into the midst of the enemy.

"It was a night of joy for the victors, as they divided the spoil. The Britons meanwhile wandered over the field, the voices both of men and women uplifted in lamentation, as they dragged off the wounded, called out for survivors, deserted their homes, and in their bitterness even set them on fire. . . . Sometimes they broke down at the sight of their families; more often they were stirred to fury. It was confirmed beyond doubt that some actually killed their wives and children, apparently from pity.

"The next day showed more clearly the extent of the victory. There was a great silence everywhere. The hills were deserted; some houses in the distance still smouldered; our scouts made no contact. Reconnaissance in every direction produced no evidence of any concerted retreat, and found no enemy concentration. Accordingly, since it was now too late in the summer for widely dispersed operations, Agricola led his army into the territory of the Boresti. There he took hostages [i.e. received the surrender of the tribe] and directed the commodore of his fleet to sail round Britain. He was given additional forces for this mission, and rumour had spread terror before him. Agricola himself led back the land forces by slow stages, so that the very leisureliness of his passing might terrorise the newly conquered tribes, to their winter stations."

The Boresti are otherwise unknown. They were perhaps a sub-tribe of one of the peoples named by Ptolemy. Their coast, where Agricola renewed contact with his fleet, must quite clearly have been well to the north, at the end of the summer's long advance; therefore, presumably, somewhere on the Moray Firth.[1] From this point, though it was now late in the season, it was not too late for the fleet to sail round the north of Britain, meeting no resistance from the cowed population; a fact which gives colour to Tacitus' claim that "Britain was completely subdued". The formal submission of the Orkney tribe was received; land still farther north was sighted, and identified with Thule, the traditional "farthest north"—perhaps the high peak of Foula. The fleet was fortunate in its weather, though the

---

[1] One thinks of the place-name Forres (mediæval Farais, etc.) on the River Varar of Ptolemy, now the Findhorn; but no certain traces of Roman penetration have so far been found west of the Spey.

oarsmen had some difficulty with the strong currents in those waters, capable, as the Orkney fishermen report, even of bearing back a ship under sail. Thoroughly puzzled, they reported that the water in those parts was "sluggish and heavy" and bad for rowing in. Finally, without incident, they made the "harbour of Trucculum", equally unknown. It must have lain at the mouth of a river called the Turk or Twrch, "the Boar", a Celtic name given to streams which dig themselves a deep bed; but no likely place-name of this type has been identified.

Calgacus was among the chiefs who survived the battle; had he fallen, Tacitus would not have failed to tell us. But as he and his comrades faced the winter, life must have seemed to offer but cold comfort. Their utmost effort, it was now proved, could indeed delay the Romans, but could not finally prevent their marching where they would in the cultivable country. The devouring or devastation of the crops, by the raids of the fleet and the march of 20,000 invaders through the east country at harvest-time, together with the loss of so many young men, meant at best semi-starvation, even for many who still survived. True, the Romans had not entered the mountain country; but the numbers of people that the still uncleared glens could support were small. Resistance in the hills, denied all access to the good agricultural land, must soon decline into banditry. It was true, too, that the Romans had withdrawn for the winter; their northernmost fort was at Cardean, not far from Inchtuthil; but it was only to be expected that they would march again in the spring, against the weakened tribes, to conscript young men for service overseas, to levy corn for their own army, to build forts and to stay.

It was only as the years passed that it became clear that Calgacus and his friends and the men who fell at Mons Craupius might have lost a battle, but they had won the war. The corn ripened again in the east country, no enemy interfering. The Romans, their high command distracted by other commitments, never did come so far north again, except once, over a hundred years later, on a glorified punitive expedition; and during the winter of 84–85, Agricola was recalled.

Chapter Sixteen

Anti-climax

AT Rome, Agricola's despatch made the news of the year. He kept it severely modest and factual. That was like him; and in any case, it was not for him, a lieutenant-governor reporting to his Generalissimo, to praise his own deeds. It was particularly important when the Generalissimo was young Domitian. But it was clear that he had won a success far more spectacular than that achieved by the emperor in the previous year—for which Domitian had permitted himself to be voted the title of "Conqueror of the Germans" by his loyal senators.

Domitian had, indeed, if we may judge by the terse and soldierly notes of the veteran Frontinus, carried out a useful and constructive piece of frontier adjustment, continuing his father's policy of pinching out the salient between the Upper Rhine and Upper Danube. After operations in the forests, during which he, too, had had to dismount his cavalry, he had run a solid police barrier, farther forward than his father's, across the base of the salient, thus circumscribing the Black Forest tribes' opportunities for cattle-raiding, and establishing Roman garrisons within striking distance of their villages. Frontinus also notes, as something worthy of comment, that in friendly country he paid for the crops destroyed on the sites where his army encamped. But the Germans, with unlimited space in which to fall back, and with no exposed coast open to sea-borne raiders, had not chosen to give him the chance of a pitched battle. Now, said gossip at Rome, here was a "real" victory; and in some senatorial circles, in which jealousy of the upstart Flavian family persisted, there was some gloating over the emperor's presumed discomfiture.

It would indeed have been no more than human if, as Tacitus assures us, Domitian was not wholly pleased at being thus outshone; but even Tacitus admits that he gave the fullest recognition to Agricola's achievement. He reported it fully to the Senate, and himself proposed or supported the proposal of the highest customary honours for the victorious general. The ancient Roman Triumph was reserved for Cæsars; but Agricola was awarded the formal rank and ceremonial robes, for state occasions, of a triumphing general, and a statue, adorned with the victor's laurel, in the city of Rome.

There was also some talk, countenanced by Domitian, of transferring Agricola from Britain to the Syrian command, that of the main eastern army, then vacant by the death of its holder; but nothing came of this; and according to Tacitus, it was a mere expedient for getting the too-successful general away from his presumably devoted army. Naturally it appears to us obvious that Agricola was of all Roman generals the least likely to attempt to make himself emperor; but, then, we have Tacitus' picture of him. Domitian could not forget by what means his father, and for that matter the great Augustus himself, had become Chief Citizen and Generalissimo. It was the nemesis of the Roman empire's revolutionary origin, of the fact that it was autocratic in fact while republican in theory, that, in the absence of any principle of legitimate succession, military rebellion or conspiracy, in the names of the Senate and People, was always possible. Many of the liquidations and purges under the Roman empire, and many of the rebellions and palace revolutions, which are at first sight so puzzling to us, arise from this fact. There was at least one real military rebellion against Domitian; and even under less suspicious emperors, mutual suspicions could arise. Once they did, the liquidation of a general might seem to an emperor, or that of an emperor to a general, a necessary act of self-preservation.

Tacitus repeats a rumour, though without vouching for its truth—once more we see that, though prejudiced, he was not a liar—that one of Domitian's confidential freedman-secretaries was despatched on a special mission to

Agricola with a sealed letter, making a definite offer of the Syrian command, to be delivered only if Agricola showed signs of reluctance to leave his army. If so, he found no need to use this lure. Their boats crossed, so the story ran, actually in mid-Channel, and the emissary returned to Rome with the seals of his packet unbroken. It is unlikely that Agricola was surprised at being superseded, though no doubt he would willingly have gone on in Britain finding a use for more time and more troops until he had either conquered the whole of the British Isles or died in the attempt. He had had seven years in Britain—as long as both his distinguished predecessors put together—and it was no novelty to relieve a general just after he had won a decisive success. It was, indeed, almost customary to give the task of "mopping up" and consolidating to a successor. This was what Vespasian had done, for instance, with both Cerialis and Frontinus, in Northumbria and Wales respectively.

Agricola proceeded quietly to Rome and, on Domitian's instructions, entered the city by night. This was to avert any danger of a popular demonstration, which might have been embarrassing. By night, too, he repaired to the Palatine; that is to say, probably, before dawn, at which hour Domitian, like other Cæsars and other Roman gentlemen, would be receiving the formal or business calls of his friends and dependants. He was received, says Tacitus, with a perfunctory kiss; that was no more than civil, from the Chief to a fellow-senator; but he was not received in conference, and without more ado mingled unobtrusively with the crowd of courtiers.

What certainly must have disappointed him, as it disappointed and angered Tacitus, was the fact that his work in Britain was left unfinished. This decision of Domitian's was not, however, due simply to jealousy. With the rise of the powerful Dacian kingdom, a serious situation was developing on the Danube. More troops were needed there, and before long the Emperor transferred thither from Britain Legion II, Adiutrix, and several auxiliary regiments including all Agricola's British cohorts and most of the veteran Batavians. In Britain itself, Wales could not be demilitarised before Hadrian's time; and the Brigantes continued to be capable of rising in fierce rebellions for another hundred years.

In these circumstances Agricola's successor (we do not know his name) evidently judged it far too risky to spread out his troops over still more territory. It is not certain whether even Inchtuthil was held. Legion XX, or the bulk of it, was needed to replace II, Adiutrix, at the nodal point of Chester; and some Scottish archæologists suspect that there was an extensive withdrawal, followed by a re-occupation which lasted until the disaster at the end of Trajan's reign. Further digging at Inchtuthil and elsewhere may give a definite answer to this question fairly soon. While Inchtuthil was held, a great boundary ditch and bank, the Cleaven Dyke (not a fortification) was dug a few miles north of it, "blazing through the forest", as Richmond has said, "the limits of Cæsar's land". Beyond it, and beyond Cardean fort in Strathmore, you were in un-friendly—very unfriendly—territory. Inchtuthil remained a powerful outpost, not, as Agricola had intended, a northern base. Thus was Britain, after being, as Tacitus says, "completely conquered"—after the Romans had landed unopposed in Caithness and the Orkneys—now "immediately let go".

However, Agricola handed over Britain to his successor, says Tacitus, "peaceful and secure"; and as the culmination of a man's work, that compares favourably with anything it usually befalls one individual to do. His last years, like those of many another famous man of action, were an anti-climax; a period of retirement, relative unimportance and some disappointment; but it must be remembered that Tacitus had definite reasons for exaggerating their gloomier side.

Agricola returned to Rome a very distinguished general, the most famous, unless it were Frontinus, then alive. He was only forty-four, and he lived in good health for another ten years; but he was never again employed. The eastern command, of which Domitian had avoided making him a definite offer, was given to another; and when, several years later, he was the senior ex-consul on the list for the proconsulship of Asia, which was the most august governorship in the empire, usually filled by seniority, and nominally in the gift of the Senate, Domitian's friends dropped hints that if he would rather not be troubled, they thought the Emperor would graciously excuse him. Agricola took the hint, and Domitian "accepted his thanks without a blush", says Tacitus indignantly. So *that* passed off quietly; and Agricola was not even paid the salary as a "consolation prize", which was a common practice. As the late incumbent had just been put to death on the Emperor's orders, the Emperor had by that time, as Tacitus says, a precedent, and Agricola a warning.

Tacitus naturally makes a great grievance of all this, and suggests rather than states that Agricola had one too; but his factual statements, here as in many other places, do not really bear out his innuendo. No doubt Agricola in retirement lived much in the past; with such a past, he would have been inhuman not to. But at the same time, we are told, he "drank deep of repose", as, after the strenuous and almost continuous service of the last fourteen years, he very well might. He was modest and approachable (but need we suppose that this was not natural to him?), and he went about with no great retinue, such as some noblemen might flaunt, so that strangers, we are told, to whom he was pointed out in the street, sometimes asked in surprise, "What? Is *that* Agricola?"

It really is not necessary to suppose that this modesty was uncongenial to him; rather it is of a piece with his whole career; though, no doubt, in an Italian environment it might seem more peculiar. But as regards Tacitus' protestations that he both was and felt very ill-used, one has to remember in what circumstances the *Life* was published. Domitian had been recently murdered and officially damned. The last years of his reign, after the unsuccessful rebellion of a general on the Rhine, had been a reign of terror; and the air of Rome was thick with charges and counter-charges of having "collaborated", having been on good terms with the monster, and of counter-claims that, on the contrary, one had been personally in danger.

Now during the terror, Tacitus had been among those

who had not merely, like the Abbé Sieyès, "lived", but had done a good deal better than that. His official career, in fact, had pursued, uninterrupted, the even tenor of its way; while Agricola, who died before the worst of the terror, had remained till his death on terms with the Emperor which were correct and outwardly friendly if not affectionate. No, Tacitus protests too much and, being fundamentally honest, supports his protestations too little. No doubt, as he tells us, Agricola's name was canvassed when an ex-consul was defeated and killed on the Danube; but there is no real reason for thinking that he would have been the best man for that front, even if "They ought to send Agricola" sounded well in the wine-shops. His military experience had in fact been unusually specialised, for a Roman general, having been exclusively British. He was therefore quite unaccustomed to mounted enemies, and to the great distances and wide fronts, with flanks often "in the air", which would be encountered in eastern Europe. So he lived out his time in quietness, on good official terms with the emperor, and even Domitian never seriously suspected him of conspiracy, though there was no lack of informers ready to accuse him, merely because he was well known. One may perhaps hazard the guess that Tacitus' mother-in-law, who was living when he wrote and who receives a rather small literary bouquet from him, missed the position of being the governor's lady more than her husband missed the camp and the road. He was not avaricious; he had a modest competence, even as senators counted it—that is to say, he was rich by any ordinary standards; and his son-in-law was rising steadily in the imperial service. Certainly the story told long after by Dio, that he died in poverty and neglect, is merely absurd.

Certainly also no senator living in Rome had any need to find life dull. One heard all the official news, at the House, and all the gossip and scandal that one wanted; and also there was continual coming and going of old friends and acquaintances, one's old officers and colleagues, and the sons and nephews and kinsmen of old friends, to and from posts in the service in all parts of the empire. The list of consuls for these years alone—a complete list for the last seven years of Agricola's life came to light recently—strengthens one's impression of the Senate as, if no longer a governing body, at any rate a very good and exclusive service club, with the chairmanship at meetings, that is the consulship, changing every couple of months among senior members, and royalty—the alarming and dangerous royalty of an autocracy—deigning to be present from time to time on occasions social or official. Priscus the law-officer was back from Britain to be raised to the consulship towards the end of 86; later he governed Upper Germany after the rebellion of 89; Tacitus may have served under him. Caristanius Fronto, once G.O.C. IXth Legion, reached that honour in 90. Roscius Coelius, whose doings as G.O.C. XXth Legion had left Agricola a difficult unit to take over, had already lived down his past sufficiently to be consul in 81. Among younger men, Valerius Paulinus, son of the knight of Fréjus who had won Provence for Vespasian, was now in the Senate, a friend of Tacitus and Pliny.

The new men of the families which had risen under the Cæsars, and not least the men of the Flavian revolution, were fast settling down to the position and functions of an aristocracy. A social event which must have taken place about the time of Agricola's return from Britain, was the marriage of Julia, daughter of Frontinus, to another member of Tacitus' and Pliny's circle, Sosius Senecio, twice consul; and one of their daughters in turn married Pompeius Falco, who took over Britain under Hadrian, just after the serious disaster at the end of Trajan's time. Frontinus himself, outliving Agricola by ten years, was consul three times, one of the last Romans, other than emperors, to be so honoured. He lived on to be an elder statesman in two more reigns; descendants of his were consuls or wives of consuls and governors of the greater provinces in every generation of the second century, and one of them, in the confusion after the murder of Marcus Aurelius' unworthy son, narrowly escaped the perils of being made emperor. About Agricola's family, the luck of discovery has given us no such wealth of detail; but Claudius Tacitus, an aged emperor who did his best and perished during the bad days of the third century, claimed descent from the historian.

In 88 Tacitus, now aged thirty-three, was prætor, and in the following year left Rome with his young wife for service abroad, perhaps on the Upper Rhine. He later published an account of the tribes of Germany which shows that he had been on that frontier at some time; and if he was concerned in the "reconstruction" after the revolt of spring 89, it would account for his extreme touchiness on the subject of the terror under Domitian. However that may be, he and his wife were not to see her father alive again; for in August 93, just when they must have been due for return home, Agricola fell sick of some form of enteric disorder and died.

It is recorded that during his last illness there were continually crowds outside his house (to hear news or read bulletins) and that the emperor himself sent both repeated messengers and also his personal physicians to offer their services. Tacitus, of course, puts a sinister construction even upon this: "Everyone agreed that he would never have been in such a hurry to hear bad news." A "persistent rumour", to which, on the other hand, Tacitus declines to commit himself, even had it that Agricola was poisoned—of course by the jealous emperor; but whoever may have suspected this, Agricola did not. He died, says Tacitus, cheerfully and bravely, rejecting any such suspicions with his last recorded breath. He named the emperor in his will co-heir with his wife and daughter; and though Tacitus has a sneer over this too, calling it "a thing no good man would ever do except for a bad emperor", he records the emperor's unfeigned pleasure at the compliment; a sign, surely, that Domitian had genuinely come to appreciate this modest and unaffected soldier.

So passed a man who had fought abuses and done his best with what he had; a man who had lived more usefully, as Tacitus claims, than leaders of ineffective conspiratorial resistance, and whose work and loyalty had taught the lesson "that great men can exist even under bad emperors". The biography ends with some lines which, while they follow closely the conventions of Roman funerary oratory, have in spite or because of this a dignity of their own:

"If there remains a place for the souls of the righteous— if, as philosophers will have it, great spirits do not perish together with the body—may you rest in peace, and turn us, your family, from weak regrets and womanish lamenting to the contemplation of your goodness, which leaves nothing to bewail or mourn. Let us honour you rather with our admiration, our unwearying praise, and so far as in us lies by following in your steps. That is the sincerest tribute, that the most fitly due from those nearest to you. That course I would commend to your widow and daughter—so to revere the memory of their husband and father, by pondering in their hearts his deeds and sayings, by clinging to the form and fashion of his character more than of his physical presence. It is not that I deprecate the making of images in marble or bronze; but like the features of men, so are portraits also weak and doomed to perish; the character of the soul is eternal—a thing which cannot be caught and expressed by art in alien matter, but by you in your life. All that we have loved in Agricola, all that we admired, remains and will remain in the minds of men, enduring through time, through the fame of his deeds. Many heroes of old will be overwhelmed by oblivion, no less than the base and the obscure; Agricola, his story told and handed down to posterity, will survive."

Epilogue

Britain After Agricola

NO one has ever claimed, then, that Agricola was a
man who dominated his epoch or altered the course
of history. Tacitus even hesitates over the question whether
his hero merits the vague designation of Great Man.
Speaking of his appearance, of which no portrait survives,
Tacitus says: "He was handsome rather than imposing.
There was no vehemence in his expression. One could
easily see in him a good man, and would have been glad to
believe him great." The writer of a biography which lies
midway between history and panegyric could hardly say
less.

The significance of Agricola lies not in his being exceptional but in his being typical; typical of what was best
in the new governing class of the Roman empire in its best
period, from the reign of Vespasian to that of Marcus
Aurelius. He was undoubtedly a man of great intelligence
and ability. Wisely under an autocracy, he showed himself
politic and obsequious, and in finding himself, almost
without choice, an early adherent of the Flavian revolution, he was, at one critical moment, lucky; but it was not
only for negative qualities that he was picked for the
command of a difficult legion at thirty and for the high
command in Britain at thirty-eight. He was also, by
Roman standards, humane. Certainly he had no doubts
about the propriety of aggressive war, at least against barbarians; but "To spare the conquered and war down the
proud" was Rome's destiny according even to so gentle a
character as Vergil, whose poetry, read, marked and
learned at school, must often have been present to him.
For anyone more pacifically minded than the national poet,
there could have been no place in the Roman service; no

place at all, indeed, in recorded first-century history, un-less as a Christian martyr.

Agricola was typical of what was best in the men who created Roman Britain, and his personal contribution to that end was no mean life-work. Not alone, but with many others—a Frontinus, a Classicianus, a Hadrian, and a host of soldiers and officials whose names are not known—he enabled British and Roman hands to build up the peace-ful and orderly south Britain of the following century. Romanisation had begun before him, he would never have denied it; and it continued after him, the faster for his personal labours. The Romanised town centres, with their baths, pillared forums, theatres and council chambers, on a scale amazingly ambitious for the size of the population, such as that of Verulamium, or that of Wroxeter with its dedication to the Emperor Hadrian, represent the fruition of his work; and roads made by the legions of the first century are prominent among the few tolerable motor-roads in use today.

Nor are the Roman roads only a material legacy. Cer-tainly their first importance—surviving even the Dark Ages, when little else survived of Roman Britain—was that of the purpose for which they were laid out, the provision of swift communications; and the destroyers of Roman Britain found them very useful. Roman law perished out of the land; so did Christianity, to be reintroduced from Rome and from the Celtic west only after generations. But the great roads must also have helped to keep alive an idea, which perhaps in the darkest days never wholly died—that of British unity. Missionaries from Rome may have fostered this idea, but there is no evidence that they intro-duced it. When Anglo-Saxon warrior kings put forward the claim, often tenuous enough, to be recognised as "Bretwalda", it is significant that they did not say "lords of the English", but borrowed the term British from their Welsh enemies and their Romanised predecessors.

As for Roman Britain in the second, third and fourth centuries, it is very easy to paint too rosy a picture; and too rosy a picture of the empire as a whole is, in fact, painted in many school histories. It is legitimate to doubt whether, even on its constructive side, the rapid and government-sponsored Romanisation of Britain was entirely and in every respect, in the time-honoured expression, a Good Thing. The vivid Celtic art, of which we have a few relics from pre-Roman Britain, was a living thing, destined to survive in the unconquered west and to come to fruition in Irish and Northumbrian work of the Christian period; but it was utterly destroyed in Roman Britain, in favour of the often very dull products of Roman provincial workshops. The prestige of Rome has, in fact, become so much of an educational vested interest that to over-praise Rome's work has become a widespread tendency. Even the Roman peace in the interior of the empire lasted not for four centuries, as is often said, but, with two brief interruptions, for about two and a half; a sufficiently notable achievement not to require exaggeration. But much less generally realised is the fact that even during the best days of the empire the prosperity and happiness, stressed by Gibbon for example, were less generally shared than Gibbon imagined. Nervousness in Rome about the possibility of a slave rising, shown already in passages of Tacitus and of Pliny's letters; nervousness on the part of the Emperor Trajan about lower-class unrest in the eastern cities; the terrible mortality, far worse than that of the free, among slaves, even the relatively privileged slaves of the civil service, shown by the tombstones of the great cemetery of "Cæsar's Household" at Carthage; widespread depopulation in Greece, to which Plutarch bears witness; these hints show that beneath the glittering surface much was far from well, even at a time when emperors and rich men still had much money to spare for unproductive building. The availability of vast sums for luxury spending also led to a steady drain of gold and silver eastwards, out of the empire, to pay for such things as pepper from India, incense from Arabia, silks from China; a trend noticed already by the elder Pliny.

The great break came in the mid third century, when emperor-making by the frontier armies set in once more and became endemic; while Germans and Persians seized their opportunities, and short-lived emperors found a short-term "remedy" for financial embarrassment in the shape of a catastrophic inflation, by successive debasements of the coinage.[1] Order was restored, especially by Diocletian (285-305), and secured by a mass of controls; a short-lived attempt to "freeze" prices, which resulted in the creation of a vast black market, and a prolonged attempt to "freeze" labour, by compelling every worker and tax-payer to follow the occupation of his father. The great landlords, especially senators, the richest of all, who did not pay the normal taxes, grew richer than ever, acquiring on easy terms the estates of lesser men who failed in the struggle; but the hard-pressed peasants broke out into repeated local rebellions, in France, in Egypt, in North Africa, which became a running sore to the struggling empire.

It was not, therefore, the barbarian invasions that caused the Decline and Fall; on the contrary, it was the decay of the empire that caused the invasions; that is, made possible a recrudescence of the migrations of the Early Iron Age.

The population of the empire steadily diminished. It was not only the senatorial class, though that did decline; largely, it was believed by Romans themselves, through plain selfishness and avoidance of parenthood. It was not even only in the towns. Depopulation affected town and country alike; *there was room* everywhere for immigrant hordes to settle. Already before 180, the Stoic emperor Marcus Aurelius was settling eastern Europeans in Austria and in Britain. Meanwhile, the eastern steppe and the northern forests had a surplus population. One is reminded of the fact that, in the mid-nineteenth century, people living under primitive conditions in the Outer Hebrides enjoyed not only a much longer expectation of life than those in the great cities, but a considerably longer one than the people of good farming districts on the British mainland. It is not primitive conditions that kill off populations, or our world would never have been populated; it is specific diseases—and also sometimes demoralisation and depression, as in animals deprived of normal outlets for their energies. But infectious diseases travel by human

[1] On this period, see A. H. M. Jones, *Constantine and the Conversion of Europe*, in this series, Chapters I and II.

lines of communication; and while Roman preventive medicine was good so far as it went, for civilised Romans were notably clean people, Roman curative medicine was still primitive. Diseases as well as armies or merchants could follow Roman roads; and the comparative isolation of the barbarian communities gave them some protection against epidemics, such as that brought back from their Mesopotamian campaign by the soldiers of Marcus.

It is a gloomy picture. One has to remind oneself that even in periods of disaster, disaster is not befalling every individual all the time, nor even every district in every generation. Also, even if the Decline and Fall had its causes far back in the social system of the early empire, it took a long time to run its course. Though "the world was growing old", as the Christian bishop Cyprian put it, Roman society had still enough vitality to take a long time to die.

This is conspicuously true in Britain. The Romanised towns, so enthusiastically promoted by Agricola and other officials, proved a weak and exotic growth. At Silchester, Calleva of the Atrebates, the area "town-planned", with its tidy grid of streets, was never even half built up; large gardens and "country" houses, even in the town's palmiest days, filled up the space within the walls. At Verulam during the third century the great public buildings grew shabby and then ruinous; at Wroxeter, the forum was accidentally burned down and was never rebuilt; the pillars of its colonnade were left lying among other wreckage in the roughly cleared street, until the wheels of the passing market-wagons had worn deep ruts in them. Such decay is not unparalleled even in the larger and richer towns of Gaul, where the walls built in the fourth century against the barbarians enclose sometimes less than one-eighth of the first-century area. But transferred to the countryside, to a form of economy of spontaneous growth and better adapted to the social and economic realities of the late empire, the Roman culture, so whole-heartedly adopted by the Celtic aristocracies, lasted on till the barbarian invasions of the late fourth and fifth centuries laid all in ruins.

This more lasting economy of the later Roman Britain

is the economy of the villas: the country houses, of Romanised British aristocrats and gentlemen-farmers. These in their turn are not so opulent as the greatest villas of Gaul, where the fortified and crenellated homes of some late Roman senators anticipate the mediæval castle. But both in France and Britain, on these broad estates, with their peasants bound to the soil (villeins, in fact), their cultivated, in the later days more or less Christian, lords and gentry, and their home industries producing manufactured goods no longer obtainable from the towns, we seem to breathe already an atmosphere of the Middle Ages.

C. F. C. Hawkes has argued that the failure of Domitian's government to make the final effort of following up Agricola's work in Scotland marked a turning-point in the whole history of Roman Britain. If the conquest had been completed, he suggests, then ultimately the country could have been demilitarised, as Spain had been. As it was, Britain never ceased to need a large garrison; three legions and actually over sixty "wings" and cohorts were found no more than sufficient in the days of Hadrian; and their maintenance was a heavy burden on a thin population with a pre-scientific agriculture. The suggestion is an interesting and a striking one; but the demilitarisation of the whole highland zone, and Ireland too if the process was to be complete, would at best have been long delayed—so long that the breakdown of peace and the imperial economy on the continent must in any case have supervened first. As it was, the indomitable Brigantes, as well as the peoples of the Scottish Lowlands when occupied, continued to rebel at intervals of about twenty years throughout the second century. To hold the whole of Scotland would have demanded either a great increase in the already costly army or the possibility of moving troops from Brigantia; and the facts show that, even as things were, the troops in Brigantia were too few for safety.

So, as it was, the south settled in peace; Northumbria remained heavily garrisoned and long restive and resentful; and the unconquered north went its own way. The Early Iron Age in most of Scotland runs on into the

Christian Dark Ages with no Roman interlude. This is not to say that the impact of Rome had no effect on these regions. Nothing is more striking about early Scotland than the wealth of late-prehistoric fortified sites, which systematic archæological exploration is only now beginning to date with precision. Fear of the Romans, and probably also a general unsettlement of society produced by the invasions and by the intrusion of irreconcilable warriors in retreat from the south, seem to have had a stimulating effect on the arts of war. Among several types of castle, the most curious of all are the brochs, that unique invention of the far northern tribes. These very strong towers, virtually impregnable to assault but too small to harbour more than a large family-group, would be at the mercy of blockade in any regular warfare; but they would afford an admirable refuge against sea-borne raiders, or in the course of feuds, such as frequently arise in a disrupted society. The age of their construction has been proved to have been in part at least contemporary with the Roman invasions; in particular, an outlying example in the Lowlands, at Torwoodlee in Selkirkshire, has been found to have been constructed on an abandoned early Roman site, and to have been demolished when the Romans reoccupied the Lowlands, as they did for some fifty troublous years, after the campaigns of Q. Lollius Urbicus about 142–143.

It was thus both a very warlike and a conspicuously anti-Roman north in which men built their brochs and hill-forts and hill-top towns, at first in constant apprehension of renewed attack; later, and especially after the Romans again and finally retired south of the Cheviot, biding their time for opportunities to raid the province; preserving the while their barbaric Early Iron Age culture, the archaic usage of chariots for chieftains (since they had neither good roads for vehicles nor thoroughbred horses for riding), and the ancient name for themselves of Britons or, in Gaelic, Cruithne; whereas the men of the south called themselves "citizens" or, more often, Romans, and devised the name "Painted Men" for the "foreigners" and "savages" beyond the pale. Against their raids the imperial administration, as problems of man-power grew more and more difficult, found no barrier to be more effective than that of the friendly Lowland tribes, whose territory they had in the end, it seems, evacuated voluntarily; the Votadini or rather Uotadini of Lothian, for instance. The facilitation of St. Ninian's mission to Strathclyde in the late fourth century was probably a last stroke of the same diplomatic policy on the part of the Christian empire.

The Roman Britain in which the first Saxons landed had thus suffered profound changes from the Britain which Hadrian visited. The illustrations to Kipling's *Puck of Pook's Hill*, which give the impression of legionaries from Trajan's Column embattled on the Wall against Saxon housecarles of the eleventh century, have indeed done no more than fix in popular imagination a view already derivable from our older school histories.

But if the empire's achievement, while it lasted, was less resplendent, if even when at peace it produced less happiness than Gibbon believed, that is no reason for denying the magnitude of the work which it did do. The prestige which it continued to enjoy, in retrospect, in its later, Christian form, even among barbarians whose fathers had known it only in decline, is itself a significant fact. The Roman roads survived as visible and important bonds of union; so did many forts, walls and other buildings, impressive in decay, as Saxon poetry bears witness. The Church, surviving among the Celts in the west of Britain and re-entering pagan England both thence and from the continent in the sixth and seventh centuries, preserved a tradition, even if faint at times, of Latin letters and of Roman order and law; and Roman rule, which so many under-dogs had hated when it was a present reality, seemed in imagination like heaven to many who had personal experience of the Dark Ages.

Note on Books

A. *Translations:*

Translations of Tacitus' *Agricola* exist by H. Mattingley, with Tacitus' *Germany*, and with introduction and notes (*Tacitus on Britain and Germany*, Penguin Books, 1948; very good); by Church and Brodribb (Macmillan, 1868, often found second-hand); M. Hutton (Loeb Library), etc.; of Tacitus' *Annals* and *Histories*, by Church and Brodribb (as above); C. H. Moore (Loeb); G. G. Ramsay (J. Murray, 1904–15, good), etc.; of Dio Cassius' *Roman History*, by E. Cary (Loeb).

B. *Modern Studies:*

Modern studies of Agricola by leading scholars will be found in *Five Men*, by the late M. P. Charlesworth (Cambridge, Mass., 1936), and by Professor I. A. Richmond in the *Journal of Roman Studies*, 1944. Among general works entitled *Roman Britain*, that of Richmond, forthcoming as Vol. I of the *Pelican History of England*, will, when it appears, be the most authoritative work on its subject. (It is necessary to say this, since a well-known classical hand-list, apparently judging books by their weight *avoirdupois*, excludes Penguins and some other cheap series on principle.) In the meantime, R. G. Collingwood's Vol. I of the *Oxford History of England* (with J. N. L. Myres on *The English Settlements*), 1937, is learned, brilliant and readable, though occasionally cavalier in its treatment of evidence, and beginning to "date." Richmond's slim picture-book, *Roman Britain* (Collins, 1947) is excellent. Oman's chapters in *England before the Norman Conquest* are now obsolete; and Winbolt's posthumous *Britain under the Romans* (Pelican, 1945), though interesting, is full of slips and best avoided. F. H. Haverfield's and Sir G. Macdonald's *The Roman Occupation of Britain* (Oxford U.P., 1925), on the other hand, keeps its freshness remarkably.

On the Roman imperial army H. M. D. Parker, *The Roman Legions* (Oxford U.P., 1928), is good; G. L. Cheesman, *The Auxilia of the Roman Army* (Oxford U.P., 1914), is a fine book, but now obsolete. The classic works in this field are German: A. von Domaszewski, *Rangordnung des Römischen Heeres*, and Kromayer and Veith, *Heerwesen und Kriegführung der Griechen und Römer*. E. B. Birley, in his *Britain and the Roman Army* (Durham U.P., forthcoming), corrects several misconceptions shared by the earlier writers. He takes a somewhat low view of Agricola.

175

On Ireland, T. F. O'Rahilly's *Early Irish History and Mythology* (Dublin, 1946) is standard; though his scepticism on many
points, salutary and antiseptic in a field which has suffered much
risky speculation, may perhaps not be found necessary by all
future scholars. Older and in part superseded by his work, but
still readable, are Eoin MacNeill's *Phases of Irish History* and
Celtic Ireland (M. H. Gill, Dublin, 1919 and 1921 respectively).
T. Raftery's *Prehistoric Ireland* (Batsford, 1951) is a good
illustrated popular survey.

C. *Topography:*

On the topography of Roman operations in Scotland much
light has been shed by archæology. See O. G. S. Crawford, *The
Topography of Roman Scotland North of the Antonine Wall*
(Cambridge U.P., 1949), and Steuart Miller, J. K. St. Joseph,
John Clarke, John Davidson and Anne S. Robertson, *The
Roman Occupation of South-West Scotland* (Glasgow; R.
Maclehose, for the Glasgow Archæological Society, 1952). For
the amazing additions to our knowledge of Roman sites—
from the street-plans of hitherto unknown forts to the very
rubbish-pits—made by air-photography, see Dr. St. Joseph's forth-
coming volume on Roman Britain in the series *Cambridge Air
Surveys* (Cambridge U.P., about 1954–5). The topographical
views taken in J. G. C. Anderson's edition of Tacitus' *Agricola*
(Oxford U.P., 1922) are no longer tenable.

For identification of Roman-period place-names, see T.
Codrington, *Roman Roads in Britain* (S.P.C.K., 1903, out of
print); Richmond and Crawford, *The British Section of the
Ravenna Cosmography* (London, Society of Antiquaries, 1949);
and the Ordnance Survey Map of Roman Britain, 2nd edition.

D. *Archæology:*

The literature of Romano-British archæology is enormous. A
good and highly select bibliography of it will be found in M. P.
Charlesworth's last book, *The Lost Province, or the Worth of
Britain* (Cardiff, University of Wales Press, 1949). The annual
summaries of new discoveries published in the *Journal of Roman
Studies* ("Roman Britain in 19—") are indispensable to the
student and should be in all libraries. Collingwood's *Archæology
of Roman Britain* (Methuen, 1930) is good, though no longer
new; so is Sir R. E. M. Wheeler's *Prehistoric and Roman Wales*
(O.U.P., 1925). Haverfield's British Academy lecture of 1906, *The
Romanisation of Roman Britain* (Oxford U.P., 4th edn., 1923) is
a classic. Brilliant summaries of results will be found in Charlesworth and others' *Heritage of Early Britain* (Bell, 1952); while
on prehistory, good introductions are Stuart Piggott's *British
Prehistory* (Home University Library, Oxford U.P., 1949), or
Jacquetta and C. F. C. Hawkes, *Prehistoric Britain* (Penguin,
1943).

E. *Sources:*

The standard edition of Tacitus' *Agricola* is that of Anderson (see above under Topography); good, but obsolescent, and sometimes cavalier in its treatment of the (admittedly very corrupt) text.

The principal Latin sources on Britain, including a few inscriptions, are conveniently collected in the late R. W. Moore's school-book, *The Romans in Britain* (Methuen, 1938).

The other sources laid under contribution for this book (apart from Tacitus and Dio) are extremely fragmentary and scattered. On Agricola's father, see Seneca's essays, Columella *On Agriculture*, the elder Pliny, *Natural History*, s.v. Græcinus in index; and the L. Julius Græcinus inscription in *L'Année Epigraphique*, 1946. On Demetrius of Tarsus, see Plutarch *On the Cessation of Oracles*, and (the same?) Demetrius' inscriptions at York. Most other individuals named can be traced through Klebs, Dessau and von Rohden, *Prosopographia Imperii Romani* (1897; new edition now in preparation); H. Nesselhauf, *Corpus Inscr. Latinarum*, Vol. XVI, 1938 (soldiers' discharge certificates), and the *Année Epigraphique* (especially volumes for 1944, 1948) for finds of more recent date. A list of consuls complete for the years 86–92 adds precision to what we knew of the careers of several of Agricola's contemporaries (see *Année Epigraphique*, 1949). The chief source for the posterity of S. Julius Frontinus is a monument in North Africa to his great-great-granddaughter Sosia Falconilla, *C.I.L.*, VIII, No. 7066. The British volume of the *Corpus* is VII; a new edition has been overdue for some thirty years. The only handy introduction to the inscriptions of Roman Britain is *The Romans in Britain: an Anthology of Inscriptions*, by A. R. Burn (Blackwell, Oxford, 1932; out of print and scarce). It contains a number of errors, but was given favourable mention by Collingwood (*op. cit.*) in his bibliography.

There is also no convenient edition in print of Ptolemy's *Geography*. The small Tauchnitz edition may occasionally be found second-hand. The best edition, though old, large and cumbersome, that of K. O. Müller, will be found in the larger classical libraries.

DATE CHART: AGRICOLA AND ROMAN BRITAIN

ROME. (Emperors in heavy type.)	BRITAIN. (Kings of Catuvellauni and Roman Governors in heavy type.)	AGRICOLA and his Family.
B.C.		
58–0. Cæsar in Gaul,	—invades Britain, 55, 54.	A.'s ancestors gain Roman citizenship through Cæsar's army?
49–6. Civil Wars; Cæsar Dictator.	**Cassivellaunus.** Commius in Berkshire.	
44. Cæsar murdered. Civil Wars.		Colony of veterans and naval base at Forum Julii.
31. Cæsar (Augustus) defeats Antony.	c. 20. **Tasciovanus.**	
A.D.		
14. **Tiberius.**	c. A.D. 5–40. **Cunobelinus** (Cymbeline).	A.'s grandfathers reach knightly rank (both procurators). A.'s father a senator.
37. Gaius.	40. Gaius plans invasion. (Fiasco).	40. A. born (13 June). His father executed.
41. Claudius.	43. Roman invasion. **A. Plautius.**	School at Marseilles.
	47. **P. Ostorius Scapula.**	
	51. Caractacus captured.	A. sees captive Caratacus?
	52. **A. Didius Gallus.**	Philosophical studies.
54. Nero. Administration of Seneca and Burrus.	c. 57. **Q. Veranius** (died).	Decides on a Service career.
	c. 58. **G. Suetonius Paulinus.**	A.'s first service in Britain.
	61. Revolt of Boudicca. **G. Petronius Turpilianus.**	62. In Rome; m. Domitia Decidiana. 63. Son born and died.
c. 62. St. Paul in Rome.	63. **L. Trebellius Maximus.** Peace policy. Wales left unconquered; Romanisation in S.E.; nationalism gaining strength among Brigantes.	
64. Great fire; persecution of Christians.		

178

68. Fall of Nero. Galba.

68. Praetor. Commission for recovery of art treasures.

69. "Year of Four Emperors." Vespasian.

69. Mutiny against Trebellius. M. Vettius Bolanus. Fall of Queen Cartimandua.

69. A.'s mother killed by looters. A. in Provence; joins Flavians.

70. Cerialis on the Rhine. Titus takes Jerusalem.

70. Agricola appointed to comd. Leg. XX in Britain.

71. Q. Petillius Cerialis. A. in Brigantian War, 71-3.

74. S. Julius Frontinus. Conquers S. Wales.

74. Governor of Aquitaine.

78. Consul. A.'s daughter marries Tacitus.

78. Cn. Julius Agricola, Governor of Britain, occupies Anglesey and purges administration.

79. Titus (acc. 23 June). Destruction of Pompeii.

79. Campaign in N.W. England and S.W. Scotland? Vigorous propaganda for Romanisation.

80. Scotland overrun as far as R. Tay.

81. Domitian (acc. 13 Sept.).

81. Consolidation behind Forth-Clyde Line.

82. Exploration of W. coast, and designs on Ireland.

83. Domitian in Germany.

83. Romans cross R. Tay. Voyage of the Usipi. 83-4. Son born and died.

84. Battle of Mons Craupius; Romans land in Orkney. A. recalled; honoured but not re-employed.

86. Beginning of Dacian Wars. Leg. II (Adiutrix) transferred to Danube from Britain.

88. Tacitus Praetor.

89. Rebellion of Saturninus on Rhine. Reign of terror at Rome.

93. Death of A. (27 August).

After 93? Sallustius Lucullus put to death by Domitian.

96. Nerva.

97. Tacitus consul.

98. Trajan.

c. 98. T.'s Agricola published.

112. T. proconsul of Asia.

c. 117. Romans lose S. Scotland.

117. Hadrian.

c. 118. Q. Pompeius Falco.

122. A. Platorius Nepos. Hadrian's Wall built.

Index

NOTES: Roman personal names are indexed under the name by which the individual is best known, i.e. usually but not always the personal *cognomen*.

Considerations of space make it impossible to include here a full gazetteer of place-names occurring in the text or maps. For further names of Roman stations on Watling Street and in Wales, the Pennines, Cumberland and Scotland, see under those headings; and for islands, see Western Isles. Names discussed are mostly indexed.